55

A.C. Rudloff
Jan 1, 1930

GEORGE C. STEBBINS:
REMINISCENCES AND
GOSPEL HYMN STORIES

GEORGE C. STEBBINS

GEORGE C. STEBBINS:

REMINISCENCES AND GOSPEL HYMN STORIES

WITH AN INTRODUCTION BY
CHARLES H. GABRIEL

ILLUSTRATED

NEW YORK
GEORGE H. DORAN COMPANY

INTRODUCTION

Confidence in the chronicler lends enchantment to his narrative. What sense of the sublimity of heaven we treasure after having gazed upon it through the lovely eighth psalm, must inevitably take its proportion of charm from the source of that mighty poem. And our enchantment is the more enthralling because of the narrative as written by that shepherd of Bethlehem.

Much that is written in this day is affectation. It solicits our attention with feeble cries of sentential puerilities and with tinsel of mawkish phantasy. It is not improbable that such has been true in any age of the past. In every cycle live men whose experience fits them and ably permits them to give voice to that which must be told.

While others may have gift for the transcription of history, for the reporting of the evolution of man's mind, for the paraphrasing of the arts and the sciences, for the execution of solid fiction, George C. Stebbins seems to be alone in qualification enabling the telling of the true story of mod-

v

ern Protestant evangelism and the development of the gospel song. For of that noble army of Christian soldiers captained by Dwight L. Moody, he alone remains to answer the last reveille.

The poet-shepherd of Bethlehem consigned his meager flock to the care of another to become "the sweet singer of Israel" whose psalms will be hallowed as long as the earth endures. Mr. Stebbins left his father's farm to spread the gospel in song around the world.

His reminiscences are not weakened by religious obliquity or sentimental conclusions. He does not merely repeat or elaborate upon that which we have often read concerning those powerful religious campaigns of half a century ago. He has something new to tell—events connected with meetings held in our own country and in foreign lands; places visited; customs of the people; incidents of travel and anecdotes of the hymns, all told in the characteristic language and modest manner of the relator.

His memoirs are vivid, instructive, interesting. His delineation of the character of Mr. Moody as he knew him, the account given of that marvelous man's last days, and of his passing, are worthy contributions to religious history.

Students of hymnology, ministers, laymen and young people of the church, owe him a debt of gratitude for this work.

I am conscious of the honor conferred on me in being privileged to write thus briefly concerning the volume now in your hands.

CHARLES H. GABRIEL.

CONTENTS

CHAPTER 1

CHAPTER 2

CHAPTER 3

CHAPTER 4

CHAPTER 5

CHAPTER 6

CHAPTER 7

CHAPTER 8

CONTENTS

CONTENTS

CHAPTER 14

CHAPTER 15

CHAPTER 16

ANECDOTES OF THE HYMNS

SONGS

PERSONAL MENTION

PORTRAITS

GEORGE C. STEBBINS:
REMINISCENCES AND
GOSPEL HYMN STORIES

GEORGE C. STEBBINS:
REMINISCENCES AND GOSPEL HYMN STORIES

CHAPTER 1

ANCESTORS; PARENTS; BIRTHPLACE; SCHOOL DAYS; DEATH OF FATHER; SINGING SCHOOL; MUSICAL AWAKENING; THE SINGING MASTER; "BONAPARTE."

My ancestors were English. Rowland Stebbins located first in Springfield, Massachusetts, in 1634, but subsequently removed, with his family, to Northampton, a town of which he was one of the founders.

It is related of him that his will was the first one to be probated in that town, and that, after disposing of household possessions and personal effects to members of his family, he bequeathed his soul to Jesus Christ.

My mother's family name was Waring, a name that is found in early English history, and among her ancestors, on her mother's side, was John Carver, of Colonial fame. There is thus some of

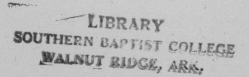

the "blood of the martyrs" and of the pilgrims in my veins.

My father and mother were born near Rensselaerville, in Albany County, New York, a little town that nestles among the northern foot-hills of the Catskill mountains. Soon after their third child was born they moved to Orleans County. There being, at that time, no railroad west of Albany, travel was made comparatively comfortable by "Packet boats," which were used exclusively for passenger service on the Erie Canal. It was by that means, therefore, that they found their way "West," as their destination was considered then to be a long way in that direction.

They located on a farm north of the Canal, midway between Rochester and Niagara Falls, which became my birthplace a few years afterward, as well as that of a sister who, beside myself, is the only surviving one of five children, of whom we were the youngest.

The eldest was a sister who died in 1863; the next a brother who passed away in 1912, honored and loved in the community where he spent his three-score and ten years, and the next a sister who died in 1861.

My father inherited much of the force and

strength of character of the Puritans, and of their loyalty to convictions, for he spent the years of his brief life in seeking fearlessly to do the will of God and to advance His cause. He was known throughout the section of country in which he spent his last years, as a Christian of great zeal for his Master, and a wise leader in all forms of Christian enterprise. I was too young to appreciate these facts then, but in succeeding years, when engaged in Christian activities myself and coming in touch with men of prominence, I began to realize the inheritance I had in my father's strong, manly Christian character; and never have I thought of him in the years that have followed, except with a consciousness of gratitude to God for such a heritage.

My mother was cast in a different mold, but was none the less valiant in faith and in good works than was my revered and honored father. She lived to a serene old age to bless her children and friends, and at the call of her Lord, whom she had served long and faithfully, passed on to the reward that only such mothers receive.

I was born February 26, 1846, in Orleans County, about fifty miles northeast of Niagara Falls, and four miles from Lake Ontario. It was then a thickly settled community, though not many years removed from what had been called the "backwoods." Our nearest village was Albion. The school district in which my father's farm was located contained about twenty-five families, the most of whom were living on the main road which ran north and south, leading, in the northern direction, to Lake Ontario.

My home was on the north-west corner of that road and one running east and west along one side of my father's farm, and diagonally opposite was the red brick school house, where most of my school days were spent. No particular incident marked my life as a farmer-boy, until my twelfth year, when two events occurred that very materially affected my life from that time onward. The first was the death of my father, which took place just before my thirteenth birthday.

The other was a Singing School, which was held that winter in the red brick school house already mentioned. No one, except those living as remote from the village as did we, can appreciate what a real event a singing school could be. It was not only the occasion for neighborhood sociability, but was the only opportunity afforded residents of isolated districts for the study of music. Hence it is no exaggeration to say that that was one of the outstanding experiences of my early life.

Up to that time I do not recall any consciousness of having any more love for music than others in the community; the fact that I possessed it to an unusual degree, however, was revealed to me during that winter, for I entered into the exercises of learning to read "Doe, Ray, Me" with the greatest interest and pleasure.

I was placed with the alto singers through the winter, and before the season ended I could sing by note very readily, which was a great delight to me.

The teacher, Dexter Manly—called "Dec" for short—was the only vocal instructor in that section of the country, and was so much in demand through the winter season that he had a school somewhere every night in the week. He was paid the munificent sum of three dollars a night, which was thought in those days to be a great salary. He was, therefore, looked upon with envy as one of the aristocrats of the country who was destined to amass a fortune.

He was a well groomed man, as we say in these days, clean-cut, clean-shaven, and quite above the average in intelligence among men of his age.

He was a man, too, of fine character, few words, and possessed a tenor voice of unusual quality and purity, which he used well, though untrained in the art. Pianos and organs were quite unknown in those days, and Mr. Manly always carried with him an "Elbow Melodion," an instrument which may be described as being much like a large suitcase, in shape. Hinges at one end allowed a steel spring to raise the other end to an angle sufficiently high to form a bellows; this was operated by the arm of the performer—the instrument lying flat on a desk. Inside the case was a set of organ or accordion reeds so placed that when the keys on the top were pressed they gave forth tones similar to a reed organ.

The keys were small, like push buttons in appearance, placed differently from organ keys, but having the same musical scale.

The instrument was used to give the pitch, or "key note" of exercises, and for playing the tunes when desired; also for accompanying solos which the teacher often sang. It was for this latter purpose that it most interested me, as he usually sang at the close of the school some song for the pleasure of his pupils. It was not only the singing of those songs by this untaught singer that so delighted me, but it revealed to me, as nothing ever had, my inborn love for music.

During those times it was difficult to realize whether I was in the body or out, so heavenly did the music sound to me.

Nor can I ever forget, as it is still sounding in the chambers of my memory, his singing the old song "Bonaparte," which gives a description of the old Hero, dead on the Island of St. Helena,

> "On a lone barren Isle,
> Where the wild roaring billows
> Assail the Stern Rock,
> And the loud breakers roar,"

being the opening lines.

CHAPTER 2

On a farm that adjoined my father's was born, two months before my birth, another George. Being so near of an age and living so near each other, it was natural that we should be much together in our early years, and the friendship thus formed in childhood continued on through youth and early manhood into life's greatest activities, and still continues, though the shadows are lengthening on our pathways.

George B. and I roamed the meadows and fields together, learned to swim in the brook that crossed my father's meadow midway between our homes, and in winter, to skate upon it. We also watched for the first ripening of the apples and peaches in the orchards.

George B. was born with a fondness for hunting, and he was given a gun and dog before he was far in his teens, and allowed to hunt at will.

34

Very often he would honor me with an invitation to accompany him on his hunting excursions, though he never seemed to feel safe when I carried the gun. The most I contributed to those hunting trips, therefore, was my company and the noise I made in walking about the woods with him, which usually brought forth some warning remarks—sometimes rather impatient—lest I disturb the game. I do not remember that we succeeded as sportsmen to any great extent, but the anticipation was sufficient to keep up our interest.

George gave me a chance to use his gun once, which should be mentioned to his credit. I fired at the first live object I saw, which happened to be a little bird that flitted about us, possibly in search of food for its young; and to my surprise and lasting regret the shot reached its mark, and the little innocent creature, one of God's messengers of joy and happiness given to earth to teach His people to praise Him, lay dead. That was the only living thing I ever shot, and from that day to this I have never forgotten the pain in my heart as I looked at that little dead bird as it lay in my palm.

In the month of April, 1861, some time after this and two years after the delightful experience of the singing school, the war between the North and South broke in upon the peace of that country-side, and from that time on to the close of the conflict, there was little else to claim the thought and attention of the people living at so great a distance from the great centers of life's activities. From nearly every household went forth one or more of the youth at the call of their country, some never to return, some to be maimed for life, and others, fortunate enough to return unscathed by shot or shell, came back not as they went, but older, and with more sober mien.

As those weary months came and went, every one watched anxiously for tidings of him whose breast was bared to the hail of death, as battles waxed and waned, and always with dread lest the tidings should confirm anxious fears.

About a year after the war began, when patriot-ism was at white heat, George B. and I discussed the possibility of enlisting a military company from among the boys of the neighborhood.   I am sure the idea originated in his fertile brain, for anything of a military character appealed to him more than it did to me.

Laying our plans, we set about the organization so earnestly that every boy between ten and fifteen years of age was interested.

George and I elected ourselves Captain and First Lieutenant, respectively, and appointed the other commissioned and non-commissioned officers down to the lowest, and strangely enough, the selections we made suited everybody, especially those appointed to office. The Captain familiarized himself with the necessary military tactics to drill the Company, then coached me and the other officers as to our duties, which enabled us to carry out his orders and instructions.

Of course, the officers must have uniforms befitting their rank, and the soldiers something that would at least pass for uniforms. The government was not back of us to provide these, and there was no money that we knew of lying around idle with which to purchase them, so our mothers came to the rescue and made them out of such material as was available.

The Captain and First Lieutenant managed somehow to get swords and epaulettes which had been handed down from the War of the Revolution —along with other insignia of office as their positions required.

The call sent out for a meeting at the brick school house for a certain Saturday evening to effect an organization was responded to with enthusiasm, and the company formed. It was arranged to begin training the following Saturday evening at the same place as soon as possible after the "chores" were done. Boys came from our school district and from adjoining districts, nearly a hundred in all, and when the officers had gotten them under discipline, their evening drills and parades became proud events to the people who came from miles around to witness our military maneuvers.

So successful was the summer's training that it was decided to call the company together for another season of training and weekly exhibitions of patriotism.

The "soldiers" responded to the second call with their former enthusiasm and entered into the training with boyish delight. The success attending the second summer was greater than the first. George B. was, of course, still Captain, and his Lieutenants were the same. We were fortunate enough to raise a military band, consisting of a snare drum, a bass drum and a fife. I was detailed to assist the "Drum Corps," at the same time retaining and performing the duties of my commission. We did considerable more parading that second year, largely due to the presence of the band. We paraded up and down the principal road; and once, I remember, we marched around the square, a distance of two miles, keeping step to the music of the band.

Although the company had "rendered great assistance to their country," it was decided at the end of the second season to disband and rest on our laurels.

So far as I can recall, there was but one out of that company of boys who joined the army during its deadly conflict to save the Union, and that was "Captain B." Before the end of the war, he arrived at military age and lost no time in offering himself to the forces at the front.

On retiring from the army he resumed his schooling at the academy in the village, and while there met the handsome and gifted young lady he afterward married.

During the campaign in which he was first elected to the presidency, Grace B., who was then about thirteen years of age, wrote a letter to Abraham Lincoln, saying she thought he would look better if he would let his beard grow—her sympathies having been aroused by thoughtless remarks of an ungainly appearance—and Mr. Lincoln answered her letter. It is well known that he let his beard grow after he became president, and it is quite among the possibilities that this was done through the suggestion of his little friend. The letter, which I have had the pleasure of seeing, is incorporated in Miss Tarbell's "Life of Lincoln," and for more than sixty years it has been the priceless treasure of its recipient—the wife of "Captain B."

Nor is this all of the story! When it became known that the train in which he was to travel from Springfield to his inaugural in Washington would pass through the home town of his little friend, he requested a political resident to find a girl by the name of Grace B. and bring her to the station on his arrival, that he might meet her. This was done, and the great-hearted Lincoln took the girl in his arms to assure her of his sincere appreciation of her solicitude for him.

Not long after George and Grace were married they went "West" to seek such fortune as awaited them, and located in one of the interior cities of Kansas, where he is still engaged.

The "two Georges" have occasionally met since those far-off days and have had delightful fellowship in recalling the exploits of their childhood and youth.

CHAPTER 3

FIRST PIANO; "SWEET EVELINA" WITH IMPROVISED ACCOM-
PANIMENT; VOICE LESSONS IN BUFFALO SIXTY MILES
AWAY; THE STUDIO; THE TEACHER; VOICE DIAGNOSIS;
"VIDER! VIDER!"; STUDIES IN ROCHESTER; TENOR IN
QUARTET; TENOR IN CHURCH CHOIR; MARRIAGE; RE-
MOVAL TO CHICAGO IN 1869; DIRECTOR OF MUSIC IN
FIRST BAPTIST CHURCH; WITH LYON & HEALY;
GEORGE F. ROOT; P. P. BLISS; H. R. PALMER; IRA D.
SANKEY; C. C. COFFIN; CHARTER MEMBER CHICAGO
APOLLO CLUB; B. F. JACOBS; INITIATION OF MALE
VOICE CHOIRS; ASSISTED SANKEY IN EDITING "MALE
CHORUS"—FIRST "POCKET SIZE" SONG BOOK.

The next event that came into those years to
relieve the routine of school in winter and farm
work in summer was the arrival of a piano in our
home, when I was sixteen years of age. It was the
first one I remember to have ever seen, and certainly the first my hands ever touched. My
mother bought it for a sister, who had a beautiful
voice, but who, unhappily, became a victim of the
"white plague" before the instrument gave her
much pleasure.

It became a delight to me and, until I left home,
afforded me the keenest pleasure, and the oppor-

tunity of learning to accompany myself in singing the popular songs of the day.

I remember well the first song I sang to chords I picked out, was "Sweet Evelina." From that beginning, being able from my knowledge of reading vocal music to get the author's idea of the changes of the harmony in his accompaniment, I soon acquired facility in improvising to the songs I sang.

That piano stands near me in my sister's home as I write, a delightful reminder of those far-off days when music thrilled me as it seldom has in these after years; and though nearly sixty years have passed since it first gladdened my heart with its sweet tones, it still responds with a semblance of its old-time harmonies.

When twenty-one years of age I began the study of the voice, going first to Buffalo—sixty miles distant from my home—once each week to a German teacher recommended as the best teacher in the city.

When I arrived at his studio, I found it to be a room about fifteen feet square with low ceiling. What space was not taken up by a square piano was filled by his own three hundred pounds avoirdupois. He tried my voice and finding I could

read music, expressed pleasure as well as surprise
and at once gave me a book of graded exercises
and set me to singing them. He also found, if
indeed it mattered to him, that my voice production
required no attention. In any case he started me
singing exercises, telling me as his first suggestion
to open my mouth wide, which I proceeded to do,
though it never seemed to me that I could open it
wide enough, for he was always urging me to open
it "Vider! Vider!"

After going to him twenty or more times I
became discouraged and went to Rochester and
studied under a celebrated teacher of voice and vio-
lin. He understood well the art of voice production, as I afterward came to know, and while he
found no occasion to change the method of tone
production I had unwittingly acquired at the outset
of my singing, he gave me exercises and instructions
that proved of great service in later years in my
own teaching.

While studying with him, I became the tenor in
a quartet choir under the direction of Herve D.
Wilkins, for many years the most prominent organist and musician in Western New York. My
Sundays were thus engaged for a year, spending
the days between at my home on the farm.

During that time I married Elma Miller, a daughter of Reverend Moses Miller, a licensed local preacher residing in the neighborhood.

There was much talk in those days of the West holding out the most inducement to a young man ambitious for a career, and as Chicago was looming up as the coming metropolis of that part of the country, I determined to cast my lot within its borders. Before doing so, however, I went there to investigate the possibilities of securing a position of some kind in line with my chosen profession. While there I made the acquaintance of Mr. Lyon, senior partner of the firm of Lyon & Healy, who, in answer to my question as to the prospects of my securing a position by which to maintain myself and family, told me that I was sure to succeed. This encouragement had much to do with my final decision to begin there the work that was to claim my thought and energies the remainder of my life.

Therefore, in the autumn of that year—1869—I made Chicago my home, going there rather blindly with no encouragement as to the likelihood of getting employment, but vaguely hoping that something would "turn up." After getting settled in a suite of rooms, that would now be called an

MRS. GEORGE C. STEBBINS

apartment, located on the corner of May and Randolph Streets, I set out to find work. Calling at principal music stores—Lyon & Healy, and Root & Cady,—I let it be known that I would accept a position in some church choir and also employment in business. As I became acquainted, opportunities occasionally offered to sing in different choirs, along with work in other lines. This went on for a year when, in the autumn of 1870, I was given the position of director of music in the First Baptist Church on the South side, one of the leading churches in the city as well as in the denomination. About that time I secured a position with Lyon & Healy, both of which came as a relief to my solicitude in the care of my family.

Some months later, however, my relations with the latter were abruptly terminated by the great fire that swept out of existence the business part of the city.

Among the musicians I met after my arrival in Chicago, aside from Dr. Root, P. P. Bliss, H. R. Palmer, and Ira D. Sankey, was Professor C. C. Coffin, who, like myself, was just beginning his career.

Professor Coffin and I were charter members of the Chicago Apollo club, which was organized shortly after the great fire and which continued for many years to be one of the most celebrated male voice organizations in the country.

Another of Chicago's older musicians that I became acquainted with in those early years is Professor C. A. Havens, organist of the First Baptist Church for a half century.

During the winter preceding the destruction of the church edifice in 1872, the society decided to change the form of its Sunday evening services to that of an evangelistic nature, to be conducted by laymen, under the direction of B. F. Jacobs, the celebrated Sunday school worker.

To add to the interest of the meetings, I organized a male quartet, principally from the choir, and as there were at that time no hymns of an evangelistic character specially written for male voices, I arranged some of the most popular gospel hymns for the quartet, which proved an attractive feature.

During that time the work of the quartet and the kind of music they were using attracted the attention of Dr. George F. Root, and he informed me that, as far as he knew, there was then no music written for male voices to hymns of that character. This being the case, and knowing of the success of the experiment, it occurred to him that, as it was a field hitherto unoccupied, it would be well to get out a book for male voices of an evangelistic nature.

He therefore edited one and used several of the arrangements I had made for the quartet. As there was no better authority in the country on subjects of that kind, he being one of the most celebrated and popular writers, as well as one of the largest music publishers, it would seem to be quite within the range of probability that the singing by that quartet of men during that winter was the means of introducing a new, and what has since proved to be a very effective and popular, custom of singing the gospel.

As an illustration of the favor with which the singing of these simple heart-songs was received in those early days there may be mentioned the very cordial and hearty reception given the quartet at the Illinois State Sunday School Convention held in Springfield, Ill., in June, 1872. Mr. Jacobs, who was the moving spirit in the convention, arranged for the quartet to conduct the singing and to sing their special selections as occasion required. This proved to be the attractive feature of the convention, and was probably due to the effectiveness of singing gospel hymns properly arranged for men's voices.

A year after the publication of Dr. Root's book for male voices, James McGranahan edited the *Male Choir,* which was used by him in his association with Major Whittle with decided success in the large choruses organized for the purpose.

Two or three years after Mr. McGranahan's book was published, I assisted Mr. Sankey in the editorial work of the *Male Choir,* a collection of specially arranged gospel songs, which volume was the first "pocket-size" song book.

CHAPTER 4

The most outstanding musical event that occurred during those early years, and, indeed, possibly in the history of our country, was the Peace
Jubilee held in Boston the summer of 1872.

Seventeen thousand singers, trained for the
purpose, were gathered from many of the States
of the Union to form a choir, and three thousand
musicians to form an orchestra. Added to these
twenty thousand singers and musicians were military bands from England, France, Germany,
Italy, Russia, Spain and the United States, and
to all these a mammoth organ of special construc-
tion swelled the volume of exultant harmonies.

To whom belongs the honor of conceiving an
affair of such gigantic proportions I am unable to
recall, but the men who carried the happy and
brilliant idea to a successful conclusion were Eben
Tourjee, the founder of the New England Con-

servatory of Music in Boston, and Patrick Gilmour, the famous band master of those years.

In spite of such a vast body of singers and musicians, under the direction of one person, the work was amazingly well done under the leadership of the two men mentioned, aided by Carl Zerahn, for many years the conductor of the famous Handel & Haydn Society of Boston, and when the first concert was given, they were ready and sang not only in magnificent volume, but with remarkable precision, which was impressive in the extreme.

I remember well that Professor Coffin was a member of the Chicago choir, as Mrs. Stebbins and I had the privilege of being; and also that I was chosen to assist in training the contingent that went on from there. Professor Coffin and I had the honor, too, of being members of the choir of three hundred men forming the male chorus.

The music sung at the various concerts was from the great masters, and consisted of selections from oratorios, famous choruses, glee clubs and national anthems. One of the interesting features of that part of the program was the appearance of Strauss, the originator and composer of the "Strauss Waltzes," and father of the celebrated musician by that name, recently visiting this country, who conducted many of his compositions to the delight of numerous lovers of his music.

The opening of the Jubilee was an overwhelmingly impressive occasion, not only to the audience who listened to the twenty thousand singers and musicians, but to the choir and orchestra as well, for the sight of thirty thousand people seated before them in the great auditorium was one never to be forgotten.

One or another of the military bands was given a place on the program of each day, which was easily the most spectacular feature of the jubilee. They not only played magnificently, animated by the laudable rivalry between them, but they were in their very best military dress and, in many cases, in imperial uniforms, which added to the attractiveness of their appearance and gave luster to their performances.

One fortunate enough to be there the day General Grant, then President of the United States, attended, and which was the climax of those wonderful days, will never forget the enthusiasm his presence created, and the ovation given him, which was "like the sound of many waters," and the acclaim of the vast audience was impressive beyond expression.

It was very fitting that he who gave utterance to the famous slogan "Let us have peace," should honor the occasion by his presence and add impressiveness to the scene. It was also most fitting that as he entered the hall, the bands struck up "See the Conquering Hero Comes," and the great audience rose to give him welcome as he modestly passed down the aisle to the place appointed for him.

Each of the seven days passed with absorbing interest in the varied programs—celebrated soloists from abroad as well as from our own country adding their voices to the Jubilee of Peace—thus maintaining to the end of the event the interest and enthusiasm of a nation in which peace once more reigned.

The two years that remained of my life in Chicago recorded no events of special interest. At the end of the autumn of 1874, having been a resident of the city five years, I resigned my position as director of music in the First Baptist Church, and removed my family to Boston with a view to pursuing my musical studies under what were considered at that time more favorable conditions.

CHAPTER 5

The winter previous to leaving my home, I was led as never before to consider seriously God's claim upon my life, notwithstanding the fact that I had a godly heritage and had lived all my life in a Christian atmosphere, attending church regularly and even singing in the choir of a country church a few miles away from home.

At that time, moreover, during the progress of a series of special meetings that were being held in the school house across the way, I declared my intention to live a Christian life.

In those years there was greater stress laid upon the necessity of an "experience" at the time of one's conversion than has prevailed in recent years, which was, perhaps, more true of the denomination to which my father and mother belonged than it was of other denominations.

I remember distinctly the impression I had when little more than a child, that people who belonged to any other denomination than "ours" had very little chance of going to heaven when they die; which was largely due to the fact, I now believe, that they did not set as much store by "experience" at the time of conversion as did ours.

I believed, as did the minister who conducted the meetings, and also those in the community who were interested, that it was necessary for one's assurance that they should pass through a period of "godly sorrow for sin," as expressed in tears of repentance, and that in due time God would answer by unmistakable evidences of His forgiveness and with an experience of joy that was wellnigh overwhelming. And I sought with deepest sincerity of heart and with repentance for my long delay in yielding to God's claims, not for a night only, but every night during the meetings, and always with a longing that the light might dawn upon me and I be given the same joyful evidences of my conversion I had so often seen in the experiences of others. But God, for some purpose I have never understood, did not give me the desire of my heart, and the meetings came to a close without the usual evidences of the genuineness of my conversion that I sincerely believed, as others did, were necessary to my peace of mind.

It was a disappointment that the work did not

seem to me, or to others, to be complete. I had
made a start, however, and God enabled me to keep
my determination to live a Christian life as best I
knew and with the light I had, which led me to
establish the custom of "family prayers" that had
prevailed in my father's home, a custom that has
never been departed from in my own in the years
that have followed.

A year or two after my removal to Chicago, I
came in contact with men who were accustomed to
deal with the "believer's assurance" from a Scriptural standpoint, and for the first time my mind
was directed away from a subjective experience
as an evidence of salvation to the word of God.
When my attention was called to the Scriptural
conditions of becoming a Christian, and also to
what was assured the believer who had complied
with those conditions, the light I had long looked for
came to me, not suddenly as I had thought, but,
as the first rays of morning light appearing on the
horizon are ere long followed by the full shining
of the sun, so the light of God's Word found in
John 1: 12; 5: 24; 6: 47, dawned upon me, dispel-
ling the darkness of doubt that had kept me so
long in uncertainty as to my standing with God.

I came to realize, therefore, that I had been

looking within, instead of to God's assuring word that "he that believeth on me hath (present possession) everlasting life," John 6: 47.

Many have stumbled, as did I, over the simplicity of the conditions upon which God gives eternal life, which are as stated in Acts 16: 31— "Believe on the Lord Jesus Christ and thou shalt be saved." However, simple as the conditions are— indeed so simple that a child may comply with them —the act of believing in the saving sense entails the greatest consequences to the believer, involving the surrender of his reliance on every other means of obtaining salvation, for "there is no other name under heaven given whereby we may be saved," and also a life of obedience to the will of God.

There are two phases to "believe" or "believing," that it is important to understand. One is believing *about* Christ what is recorded of Him in Scripture as to His life and earthly ministry, His work in redemption, His death and resurrection and ascension—all of which is essential; and the other is believing *on* Him. It is, therefore, only as one believes on Him in this latter sense that he comes into saving relation with Him. In the former sense one may believe the "record God gave of His son," and yet live apart from Him; in the other sense, there is a vital union with Him—the all-essential condition for the possession of the life He died to give.

I have been led to dwell on the foregoing, because I have learned in dealing with inquirers in my evangelistic work that, in some phases, my experience at the time of my conversion is typical rather than exceptional; for the desire to have an experience that testifies to one's feelings or consciousness at the outset of the Christian life, is well nigh universal.

Nor is this desire confined to those seeking to know the way of life, but it is not infrequently found among professing Christians who are not well grounded in God's plan of salvation.

A beautiful and rather striking comment upon the subject of "Believing," by Anne Johnson Flint, is here appended as an illustration of what the attitude of every child of God should be, and of that which alone brings one into the "rest of faith" so essential to the Christian's highest usefulness.

> "I believe God that it shall be even as it
>   was told me," Acts 27:25.
> "I believe God"—but do I? Am I sure?
> Can I trust my "trusting" to endure?
> Can I hope that my belief will last?
> Will my hand forever hold Him fast?

Am I certain I am saved from sin?
Do I feel His presence here within?
Do I see the answer to my prayers?
Do no fears my confidence assail?
Do I know my faith will never fail?

"I believe," ay, I do! I believe
He will never fail me, and I know
His strong hand will never let me go.
Seeing, hearing, feeling, what are these?
I believe in Him and what He saith;
I have faith in Him, not in my faith;
That may fail, to-morrow or to-day,
Trust may weaken, feeling pass away,
Thoughts grow weary, anxious or depressed;
I believe God, and here I rest.

CHAPTER 6

On leaving Chicago to make my home in Boston,
which occurred in November of 1874, five years
after leaving the old homestead farm, Mr. B. F.
Jacobs, in whose large Sunday School and Bible
Class I had led the singing for four years, gave me
letters of introduction to three of his Boston friends
—Dr. A. J. Gordon, pastor of the Clarendon
Street Baptist Church of that city, one of the
ablest and best loved ministers in his denomination, and composer of the music of the well-
known hymn, "My Jesus, I Love Thee"; Mr.
J. S. Paine, a wealthy merchant, life-long friend
of Mr. Moody, and ever after a kind and valued
friend to me; and Mr. Eben Shute, a business

man, and well known in New England as a Sunday School worker.

I gave the letter addressed to the latter first, and I will never forget the expression on his face as he read it. I thought I had never seen so beautiful a smile as wreathed his face, and it would be impossible to say how much good it did me. Being a total stranger in the city, with no certainty of securing a position of any kind, to be greeted so kindly and with such an evidence of pleasure on his part was an experience the memory of which has never lost its fragrance.

I presented the other letters in due time and was greeted in each case most cordially. My uncertainty as to a position was soon relieved, for within a week of my arrival in Boston I was engaged to lead the singing in Dr. Gordon's church and in his Sunday School, of which my delightful friend was the very efficient superintendent for many years.

The year and two months of my service in that church, leading up to the first of January of 1876, when my engagement as director of music in Tremont Temple began, was a very happy experience, as friendships were formed that have been cherished among the most valued of my life. As a memento of the fellowship with those friends, there hangs above my desk, as I write, a large steel engraving of one of the most famous works of art, that was a gift to me from the Sunday School of Dr. Gordon's church, on my going to another field.

During my rather brief residence in Boston—a little less than two years—I had, besides my regular duties in the Temple, occasion to conduct the singing for Sunday School and other religious conventions, special meetings, mid-week Bible classes, etc., at which times my voice was in considerable use for solo purposes, as the songs Mr. Sankey had made famous across the sea were in constant demand. I was thus kept in touch with a considerable part of the religious activities in New England, and with work along lines which were to engage my efforts and time the remainder of my life. I little anticipated then that it was in a measure preparing me for that work, and still less did I think I was to enter upon it so soon.

In August of that year there was a gathering of friends at one of the near-by seaside resorts for Bible study and exposition, among whom were Dr. James H. Brooks of St. Louis, Dr. W. J. Erdman, Major Whittle, and others. Having known the latter for many years and not having seen him for some time, I took occasion to attend one of their services, which was the first time I remember to have met Dr. Brooks, who greatly impressed me with his forceful personality. He stood over six feet in height, well proportioned, and with a strong, intellectual face; all of which stamped him as a man of commanding presence.

He gave an informal exposition that afternoon which showed him to be a man of extraordinary ability as an expositor of the great fundamentals of Christianity. He was also known as a believer in the premillennial return of our Lord, and a great defender of the "faith once for all delivered to the saints." That conference was the first, I believe, of the summer conferences known as the "Premillennial Conference," and in the after years as the "Niagara Conference," held at Niagara-on-the-Lake.

Major Whittle invited me to accompany him to Northfield to spend Sunday with Mr. Moody, which I did, and where I assisted in the services Mr. Moody had arranged to hold in the little New England village church in which his townspeople first heard Mr. Sankey and himself on their return, the summer before, from the work in Great Britain that had given them such fame. It was in that church where, four years later, was held the first conference which in subsequent years was to make Northfield a household word throughout Christendom.

It was from the steps of that church, too, that one summer evening, when such a crowd had gathered that it was necessary to hold the service outside the church, Mr. Sankey sang his famous hymn: "The Ninety and Nine," and which was the means of converting a man who heard him sing it, although that man was quite two miles away and across the Connecticut River. It was a still summer evening when the song was sung and Mr. Sankey, sitting at his organ with the front of the church at his back acting as a sounding board to send his voice so great a distance, rang out that impressive story of the lost sheep so clearly and distinctly that the man sitting on his door step on the western bank of the river caught the sound of the voice and the message of the song, and awoke to the fact that he was one of the lost sheep and that the Shepherd was seeking him, with the result that he was soon found of Him and brought into the fold. The man lived to become an official member of the church from the steps of which the sweet song was sung.

It is said of him that when dying, some years

afterward, he heard Mr. Sankey singing again—this time from the new church building which stood not far from his home at that time—an impressive coincidence and one that must have awakened in the mind and heart of the dying man very precious memories.

At the services I was privileged to attend there on my first visit to Northfield, the church was crowded with people from the village and adjacent neighborhood who had come to hear their fellow townsman. Mr. Moody had me lead the singing and play the cabinet organ which stood on a low platform just in front of the pulpit.

Aside from the impressive address of Mr. Moody, there was nothing to fix that part of the service in my mind especially, except a discordant sound I kept hearing during the singing, which I at first thought was caused by something wrong with the organ. I determined to ascertain if my suspicions were well founded, so when there was an interval between verses, I listened to see if there might be one of the notes of the organ sounding when it ought to be silent, and found the discords were not from that source.

I was not long in doubt, however, for I soon heard the voice of Mr. Moody singing away as heartily as

MAJOR D. W. WHITTLE

P. P. BLISS

you please, with no more idea of tune or time than a child. I then learned for the first time that he was one of the unfortunates who have no sense of pitch or harmony, and hence are unable to recognize one tune from another or to sing in unison or harmony with others. I came to realize in after years, however, that in spite of that defect, he, as I have known to be the case with others similarly affected, loved the sound of music, and I have seen him at times bowed under the power of an impressive hymn as I have known no other to be.

The few days spent with the great evangelist in his home were memorable days and never to be forgotten. I was permitted to see him at close range as I had never before, and I found him to be in every essential human, with no signs of a halo around his head as one is apt to imagine surrounds the head of all great people; but rather to be unaffectedly simple in his every-day life and association with others. As a husband he was the most thoughtful and considerate of men, and as a father the idol of his children and their most interesting and delightful companion and play-fellow. The impressions he often gave in public, that he was at times lion-like in his mastery of assemblies and unapproachable, was quickly dispelled when seen in his home, for there he was the very antithesis of that. In the home of his friends also, I found in after years, he was ever gentle, thoughtful and considerate.

So he was during those days spent in his home in Northfield. The incident that occurred during my stay that stands out in my memory as illustrating his thoughtfulness of others, was inviting people to his home to hear me sing. He took me in his buggy one day and drove about the country, and as we came to a farm house, he would stop and ask the people to come to his home on a certain day to hear some singing. The afternoon set for the entertainment proved to be one of the hottest days in August, which, however, did not deter the people from coming. They had a feeling that an invitation from their celebrated friend was like the command of a king, and one not to be declined.

At all events they came in large numbers and crowded the largest room available in his home. The organ I used to accompany myself stood by an open window, by which Mr. Moody sat and selected the hymns for me to sing. He kept me there for an hour in spite of the fact that he saw the heat was having a "melting" effect upon me, and though he himself could not very well endure it. I have sometimes thought he did this partly because he liked to see me perspire, as he never seemed to enjoy anything in the way of fun quite so much as to have a joke on his friends—a characteristic that was very pronounced in early life, and which never quite left him even when the weight of years and many cares were resting upon him.

Before my visit came to an end Mr. Moody broached the subject of my entering evangelistic work, giving me to understand that I would be associated with him and Mr. Sankey, and that my time would be subject to his disposal. After prayerful consideration I decided to retire from the pursuit of my profession, involving though it did the sacrifice of the ambition I had cherished for years. There seemed to be a leading, though not so clear to me at the time as it afterward appeared, that a larger field for the use of such talent as I possessed had opened to me, and that I should enter it. At all events the decision was made then, and steps taken to sever my connection with Tremont Temple and other pursuits that were engaging my attention, to devote myself henceforth to evangelistic work.

This decision marked the end of seven years that had intervened since leaving the home of my early years; the end also of the second period in my history, and the beginning of the third, which was to be the last and longest.

CHAPTER 7

BEGINNING OF ASSOCIATIONS WITH MOODY AND SANKEY;
ORGANIZING CHOIR FOR WORLD'S FAIR MEETING IN
CHICAGO; P. P. BLISS; FARWELL HALL; WITH GEORGE
C. NEEDHAM; CHARLES INGLIS; LAST VISIT WITH MR.
AND MRS. BLISS.

Thus began my association with Moody and Sankey, men upon whose ministry God had set His seal in a remarkable way, and which was destined to last throughout their lives.

The first work assigned me by Mr. Moody was to organize a choir to assist in a three months' evangelistic campaign he and Sankey were to conduct in Chicago, beginning the first of October, 1876. On the first of September, accordingly, the work was undertaken. An appeal to the churches of the city for singers brought a very hearty response, and a chorus of about one thousand voices was secured.

Rehearsals were well attended, and in addition to the more familiar hymns we gave attention to the newer songs of P. P. Bliss, such as "What Shall the Harvest Be," "Almost Persuaded,"

"Go Bury Thy Sorrow," and others. "Knocking, Knocking, Who Is There," and other compositions of Dr. Root were also very impressively sung by the large choir. "What Shall the Harvest Be" became a favorite immediately and was often sung.

During the four weeks devoted to organizing the choir, and familiarizing them with the work they were expected to do, I was given accommodations at a hotel in the center of the city, which was headquarters of the committees having the meetings in charge; and in that way I came in touch with many of the men prominently identified with the movement. Among them was the author of the hymn, "It Is Well with My Soul," Mr. H. G. Spafford, a man of unusual intelligence and refinement, deeply spiritual, and a devoted student of the Scriptures.

One day Mr. Bliss, who was also entertained at the hotel, came to my room with the first draft of the musical setting he had made to Mr. Spafford's words, and sang it for me; taking occasion also to call my attention to some progression in the harmony.

It was at that time he handed me the words to the hymn known as "Fully Trusting," and suggested that I write music for them. This I did, and the hymn was incorporated in Gospel Hymns No. 3, published a year or two afterward. "It Is Well With My Soul," was published at the same time, and, immediately coming into general use, proved to be one of the strongest and most useful of gospel hymns.

The meetings conducted in Chicago by Mr. Moody were held in a permanent brick structure erected in the center of the business part of the city and had seating capacity for ten thousand people. It had high ceiling, large galleries, remarkable acoustics, and was admirably adapted for music. It was known as Farwell Hall.

I was appointed to assist George C. Needham in his work in Oshkosh, Wisconsin, and later, with Charles Inglis, of England, I was sent to one of the smaller churches of South Chicago. On entering the railway station on my way to this second appointment, I found Mr. and Mrs. Bliss waiting for the train I was to take.

It so happened that Major Whittle and Mr. Bliss were to begin a series of meetings in Peoria, Ill., at the same time our meeting began in South Chicago.

While bidding good-by to Mrs. Stebbins and our son, then a small boy, Mr. and Mrs. Bliss were reminded of their two boys in the home of friends in Rome, Pennsylvania, and tears came to their eyes.

After leaving Chicago Mr. Bliss fell asleep, with his head resting on his wife's shoulder. He was still sleeping when my destination was reached. As I rose to pass out, I said to Mrs. Bliss, "Don't disturb him." She replied: "Oh, yes! He would be disappointed if he did not say good-by." As he wakened and realized I was leaving, he followed me onto the platform with kindest wishes and parting words.

This proved to be the last time I saw him, for he and Mrs. Bliss, at the conclusion of the meetings at Peoria, went to their children to spend the holidays, and on their way back to Chicago, a few days later, they met their tragic death at Ashtabula, Ohio.

CHAPTER 8

During the fortnight following my good-by to Mr. and Mrs. Bliss, Mr. Inglis one day sang to me the hymn known as "Crown Him" ("Look ye saints, the sight is glorious!") As he sang it entirely from memory, I wrote down the melody.

Mr. Inglis did not know who composed or where he had heard the tune which, evidently, was of English origin. The song was published in the next number of "Gospel Hymns," and became one of the popular numbers in that collection. It was also included in Mr. Sankey's English hymn book and was widely used in that country. Yet no one has laid claim to its authorship.

Mr. Inglis, since that time, has visited this country nearly every year in the course of his evangelistic work; and although "living on borrowed time" (as I often heard Mr. Moody say of those who had lived beyond the allotted span of life), he is still (1924) preaching the gospel in this country as well as at home.

73

Following my appointment with Mr. Inglis and a short engagement with Mr. Needham at Fort Wayne, Indiana, I went to spend the holidays with my mother and brother who were still living in the old homestead. During this short vacation a very severe storm came on which blocked all the country roads and interrupted railway traffic. It was while thus situated that I received a telegram from Mr. Moody advising me of the death of Mr. Bliss and wife, and requesting me to return to Chicago at once to join Major Whittle in following up the work he and Mr. Sankey had just closed. I made my way with difficulty to the railroad, and after some twenty-four hours of slow progress, reached my destination, to find the whole city greatly moved by the disaster at Ashtabula. The churches especially were stirred through the prominence of Mr. Bliss' songs.

At the close of that follow-up campaign, conducted by Major Whittle, I went on to Portland, Maine, to join Mr. Needham in a series of evangelistic services.

On my return journey to Chicago I spent a few days with Moody and Sankey in their great work in Boston.

Aside from the blessings that attended the meetings the remainder of the season in Maine there is no incident worthy of note, save that it marked the practical beginning of my writing; for, while I had only two hymns to my credit for that spring's work, I found my mind turning more to the exercise of any gift I might possess in that line than ever before.

CHAPTER 9

In the following August I assisted Dr. Pentecost in a series of summer campaigns, the first of which was held in Worcester, Mass.

During those meetings, one of the subjects preached upon was the "New Birth." While presenting the truth, enforcing it by referring to various passages of Scripture, Dr. Pentecost quoted our Lord's words to Nicodemus, "Verily, verily I say unto you, ye must be born again," John 3: 3-7. It occurred to me that by taking the line "Verily, verily, I say unto thee," from the third verse, and putting it with the line, "Ye must be born again," and by transferring the word "I" from the middle of the first line to the beginning, so it would read, "I verily, verily, say unto thee, Ye must be born again," those passages would then fall into rhythmical form, and by the use of some repetitions could be made available for a musical

76

setting, and also for a chorus to a hymn, if some suitable verses could be found.

I had long been impressed by the fact that that truth lay at the fóundation of God's plan for the salvation of men, and that it was of the greatest importance that it should everywhere be made known. It also came to me with special force that a good hymn, using those lines as a refrain, would be a means of emphasizing that truth and thereby doing great good. I spoke to Reverend W. W. Sleeper, one of the pastors of the city who sometimes wrote hymns, of my impression and asked him if he would write me some verses on the subject. He acted at once upon my suggestion and soon after came to me with the hymn that bears his name. Before the meetings closed a musical setting was made, and when "Gospel Hymns No. 3" came out the song was sent on its mission carrying the solemn message to the hearts and consciences of men indifferent alike to their danger and to God's claims upon them.

The following incident is of interest as showing not only the magnetic attraction of song, but its power in carrying a message to the heart, and its tendency to awaken the careless to a sense of need.

"One evening in November, 1886," said the Superintendent of a boys' school, "I was walking along a street in St. Joseph, Missouri, when I saw before me a great crowd gathered around a door. On approaching, I discovered it to be the entrance to the Young Men's Christian Association hall. In the doorway stood some young men singing. Just as I came near enough to hear, they began:

'A ruler once came to Jesus by night,
To ask Him the way of salvation and light;
The Master made answer in words, true and plain,
"Ye must be born again." '

CHORUS:
'Ye must be born again,
Ye must be born again;
I verily say unto you,
Ye must be born again!'

When they came to the chorus, the sword of the Spirit entered my soul. It seemed to me that I was brought face to face with the Lord Jesus. There on the street, while the song was being sung, I asked Him to teach me how to be born again, and He did. I accepted an invitation to the service of the evening, and after that service, for the first time in my life, I publicly acknowledged Christ as my Savior. I have always considered that it was through the influence of that hymn that I was awakened. Many times have I thanked God for the song, as well as for the courage He gave to His disciples to sing it in that public way."

Some years after this hymn was written, Mr. Sleeper sent me the verses of the hymn "Jesus, I Come" ("Out of my bondage, sorrow and night"), which is a hymn of rare excellence, from any point of view, and one in which the author might properly have taken great satisfaction, for he lived to know it was very extensively used in foreign lands as well as in his own country.

Besides this engagement with Dr. Pentecost I had others, which made my first summer after entering the new field of activities a very busy one. Trailing each other closely came the "Sunday School Parliament" at the Thousand Islands; conventions in Montreal, Quebec, New Hampshire and Massachusetts; Y. M. C. A. State conventions, services of song in various cities, and meetings with Dr. Pentecost in Nova Scotia and Maine.

In October I assisted both Reverend William Rainsford and Evangelist L. W. Munhall in meetings which were held in the tabernacle Moody and Sankey had used for their great campaign the winter and spring preceding—a fortnight being given to each series of meetings.

CHAPTER 10

My next engagement was with Dr. Pentecost
in special meetings in his own church in Boston.
During this engagement the "Green Hill" was
written, to be sung as a quartet by three prominent
church soloists of the city and myself, at a special
service.

On the evening appointed a severe storm pre-
vented the three friends coming, and most of the
usual congregation. The service was held in the
lecture room of the church, and I ventured to sing
the new song alone. There seemed to be little or
no impression made by it, and as no one did me the
honor to refer to it, I concluded it was a failure.

Two months thereafter—January, 1878—while
engaged with Dr. Pentecost in a series of meetings
Mr. Moody had arranged to follow those he and
Mr. Sankey had conducted in Providence, Dr.
Pentecost said to me one day:

"George, where is that 'Green Hill' you sang in my church?"

I answered: "The music is in my head, but the words I left in Boston." Some time afterward I chanced to find them and said to the Doctor, "I can sing the 'Green Hill' for you now, if you like," and he replied, "I wish you would."

Great interest had been awakened by Mr. Moody's meetings, and it kept up during the work of Dr. Pentecost, hence there was an atmosphere that was sympathetic and responsive to both sermon and song. The services were held in Music Hall—the largest auditorium in the city—and at the time fixed upon to sing the new song a very large number of people were present. Conditions, therefore, were favorable and that it was the means of a blessing may be judged by the fact that from that time on to the end of the series, some weeks later, there were few services when from one to a half-dozen written requests for its repetition were not sent to the platform.

In this connection it may be of interest to relate the origin of the music of "Evening Prayer."

During the first part of my term in charge of the music in Tremont Temple, Boston, it occurred to me to write music to a verse suitable for a response after prayer—it being the custom to sing such at the morning service—and the music, since known by the title mentioned above, was written.

Two years afterward, while these meetings in Providence were in progress, I was reminded of that music, and the thought came to me that if I could find a hymn suited to it, it might be worth publishing. With this in mind I began looking through such church hymn books as came to my hand, and "Savior, breathe an evening blessing" caught my eye, and finally was chosen. I arranged to have a male choir of 200 voices sing the music as set to the beautiful hymn, and to my gratification found they were admirably suited to each other. Since then the hymn has been used in many gospel hymn books and church hymnals, both here and abroad. It has been used, also, in St. Paul's Cathedral, in London.

It was during this engagement that I wrote the music of three of my songs—"I've Found a Friend," "Must I Go, and Empty Handed" and "What Must It Be to Be There." These compositions, with "Evening Prayer" and "Green Hill," were first published in "Gospel Hymn No. 3," the first number of that series with which my name was identified as associate editor.

Of the "Green Hill" Mr. Sankey wrote me—
"While holding meetings with Mr. Moody at
Cardiff, Wales, in 1883, I visited the ruins of Tin-
tern Abbey with Professor Henry Drummond,
and sang this hymn, which Mr. Drummond said
was one of the finest in the English language." A
number of years later I sang it on the "Green
Hill," believed to be Calvary, outside the walls of
Jerusalem.

Mrs. Alexander—the author of the words—was
the widow of an Irish clergyman. She published
the hymn in her "Hymns for Children" in 1848.
Mrs. Alexander, who was born in Ireland, wrote
some four hundred hymns and poems for children.

An incident regarding "I've Found a Friend"
is related by Mr. Sankey also. "We were holding
a prayer meeting in a lodging house," says a minister of Nottinghamshire, England, "when a young
man came into the meeting in a fun-seeking manner. We sang, prayed, and read out of God's
Word, and then the young man asked if we would
sing a hymn for him. He chose 'I've Found a
Friend.' When we had sung one verse he began
to shed tears, and I am glad to say that he gave his
heart to God through the singing of that beautiful
hymn. The next morning he left the place, but

before leaving he wrote me a letter, of which I give these extracts.

" 'I asked you to sing that hymn, because it was the favorite of my sister, who is waiting for me at the gates of heaven. I have now promised to meet her there. Try to always think of me when you sing that hymn.' "

Of the hymn "Must I Go, and Empty Handed" the author of the words, Reverend C. C. Luther, relates that it was inspired by the remark of a dying young man, who said, "I am not afraid to die; Jesus saves me now, but, oh! must I go empty handed?" During our stay in Providence, Mr. Luther handed the words to me, and the music was written shortly afterward. An incident is told of the singing of the hymn in Essex, England, in a morning service attended by a godless youth. At the third verse —"Oh, the years of sinning wasted," etc., the young man was so forcibly impressed that he went home .miserable and was unable to eat his dinner. In the afternoon he went to a Bible class for working-men, conducted at the other end of the town. As he entered, the same hymn was being sung. He was so moved thereat and so impressed by the co-incidence that it resulted in his conversion and in his leading a consistent Christian life thereafter.

Of the hymn "What Must It Be to Be There," Philip Phillips, the "Singing Pilgrim," said, shortly before he died at Delaware, Ohio, "You see that I am still in the land of the dying; why I linger so long is a problem. The precious Savior is more to me than I ever expected when I was well. Often during the night I have real visions; I walk on the banks of the beautiful river and get glimpses of the bright beyond. The lines that come most often to me are these:

> " 'We speak of the land of the blest,
> A country so bright and so fair,
> And oft are its glories confessed,
> But what must it be to be there?'

Blessed be God! I shall soon know. What a singing time we will have when we get there!"

I was leaving the auditorium at Northfield one Sunday evening some years ago, when Miss Helen Knox Strain, a missionary on leave, told me an incident connected with "Evening Prayer" that happened during the Boxer movement in China. Her story was so impressively told that I asked her to write it out in full for me, as it rarely falls to the lot of a hymn to be sung under such trying and well-nigh tragic circumstances. The account, as she wrote it, is as follows:

"The Woman's Union Missionary Society has a magnificent work just outside the city of Shanghai. No harm had come to us up to this time, but serious threats and rumors were rife; we dared not so much as put our heads out at night, though forty little soldiermen played at keeping us safe. Our missionaries have two centers at that place, and they meet often for prayer and consultation. At this particular time the rumors were frightful, and the threats to burn our homes that very night were so distressing that our meeting was a memorable one. Separated from home and from friends, facing death in a far-off land and full of tenderest feelings, we lifted our hearts in song.

" 'Though destruction walk around us,
   Though the arrows past us fly,
   Angel guards from Thee surround us:
   We are safe if Thou art nigh.'

Out of the storm each soul, renewing its strength, mounted up with wings as eagles and found peace in the secret of His presence. Our Savior breathed, in very deed, an 'evening blessing' upon us, the fragrance of which remains to this day. The last verse of the hymn,

" 'Should swift death this night o'ertake us
   And our couch become our tomb,'

was omitted, as it seemed too probable that such it would be. We wanted only to think of the safe-keeping, and such, thank God, it proved to be."

CHAPTER 11

Many interesting and touching incidents and
many histories are revealed by awakened consciences, and stories of blighted lives whispered
into the sympathetic ears of Christian workers.
Dr. A. J. Gordon related a beautiful incident that
took place during Moody and Sankey's great meetings in Boston, referred to in the foregoing chapter. Mr. Moody arranged to have his inquiry meetings held in Dr. Gordon's church, which stood near
the tabernacle. One night Mr. Moody found a
mother with her small child in the inquiry room
deeply interested in becoming a Christian, and he
asked Dr. Gordon to sit down and help her. While
so doing, the baby cried frequently. A big man
who had been greatly blessed in the meetings, and
who had a desire to be of some help, noticed Dr.
Gordon's effort to help the mother of the restless
child and, stepping up to him, said:

"I do not know how to help any one to become

88

a Christian, but if the mother will let me, I will care for her child while you talk with her." The mother consented, and Dr. Gordon said it was a beautiful sight to see that strong man carry and quiet the babe, in his desire to do something for his Master.

A very interesting incident of another nature occurred during these meetings. There came into one of the inquiry meetings a middle-aged man, beside whom Dr. Pentecost sat down to ask if he could be of service to him. The man acknowledged that he was interested in becoming a Christian and would be glad of help. During the Doctor's explanation of the plan of salvation the man suddenly exclaimed: "Hold on, Pentecost, I'll go home and talk with Brown about it," and, taking his hat, left the room. The man came a second time, and again the Doctor approached him. Again, as on the first occasion, the stranger declared: "I'll go home and talk with Brown about it," leaving as unceremoniously as before.

Later on he came a third time, and a third time Dr. Pentecost sat down beside him. As on both previous occasions, it seemed the inquirer had gotten some new thought he wanted to think over, and was on the point of leaving when the Doctor asked:

"Who is this Brown you speak of?" The man replied, "It is no one but myself; I am in the habit of talking over my business matters with an imaginary man, and I call him Brown." The man went away, but before the campaign closed, he came back and told his experience.

"One night I couldn't sleep for thinking over the matter," he said, "and finally 'Brown' suggested: 'Pentecost says it is only to believe, just to trust Him. Do you see that peg on the wall?' 'Yes,' I said. 'Do you think it would hold your hat?' asked Brown. 'I'll get up and see,' I replied, and the moment I saw my hat on that peg the light dawned upon me. Then Brown said to me, 'Now that you are a Christian, you will have to reorganize your business!' "

During that series of meetings, Dr. Pentecost had a very amusing, as well as surprising, reply to the question he was in the habit of asking—"Are you a Christian?" Walking up the broad aisle in one of our after meetings asking the question here and there, he saw ahead of him a rather dignified looking lady sitting next the aisle, and when he accosted her with: "Madam, are you a Christian?" she replied instantly, "No, sir, I'm an Episcopalian."

Our next work was at Hartford, where the interest awakened by Moody and Sankey in their campaign during the early part of 1878 was maintained unabated by the follow-up sermons of Dr. Pentecost. The rink that had been used during those memorable days continued to be crowded night after night for weeks.

The "Green Hill" and "Evening Prayer," sung by the large male choir, were called for frequently.

Mark Twain came to the meetings occasionally, but so far as is known he manifested little interest in them or the work accomplished during the winter.

After Moody and Sankey had finished their work in New Haven, Dr. Pentecost followed, as in other cities. The meetings in New Haven were also held in a rink and attended by throngs of people who had been awakened by the great evangelists. No incident worthy of notice occurred in this meeting, except the popularizing of "Wonderful Words of Life." Nearly two years previous to that time, Fleming H. Revell, the publisher, handed me a copy of the first issue of a Sunday School paper called "Words of Life," and stated that Mr. Bliss had written a song especially for use therein.

I carried that song through two seasons of evangelistic work, never thinking it possessed much merit, or that it had the element of special usefulness, particularly for solo purposes. It occurred to me to try it one day during the campaign in New Haven, and, with the help of Mrs. Stebbins, we sang it as a duet. To our surprise the song was received with the greatest enthusiasm and from that time on to the close of the meetings was the favorite of all the hymns used. As an illustration of the hold it got upon the people all about that section of the country, I received a letter from the Secretary of the Connecticut State Sunday School Association offering me what seemed an absurdly large sum of money, if I would, with Mrs. Stebbins, come to the State Convention and sing that one song.

So far as I ever learned the song had neither been published in any hymn book prior to that time nor used in meetings anywhere. It was used in "Gospel Hymns No. 3," and at once became one of the most popular songs in Evangelistic Services and in the Sunday Schools of the land.

That was a striking illustration of the unreliability of prophecy regarding the usefulness of a hymn, before it is submitted to the public; for it is, after all, what the people like or dislike that decides. I have failed as a seer in that line enough times to take out of me all the conceit I ever had concerning my prophetic abilities.

CHAPTER 12

IN DETROIT; CONFERENCE AT NORTHFIELD; CHICAGO; MIN-
NEAPOLIS; "SWEET WILLIAM"; GENERAL CUSTER'S
GREYHOUNDS.

In the beginning of the year 1880 Dr. Pentecost
conducted a series of very successful services in
Detroit, in which there was a great awakening
among church members as well as among non-
church-goers. During those weeks I found time
to give to composition, and the most notable result
of that phase of my work was the music to Dr.
Horatio Bonar's beautiful hymn, "Beyond the
Smiling and the Weeping." Mrs. Stebbins and
I began singing it at once and found it to be one
of our most useful hymns. I shall not forget how
the solemnity and truth of the words impressed
singers and listeners. Especially do I recall the
many times it was sung the following summer at
Northfield, during the first conference Mr. Moody
called for the deepening of the spiritual life. The
conference was held in the old Congregational
church, and was most impressive, and probably the

94

most fruitful, of all the long line of great conferences held there since.

Mr. Moody had given expression to his sense of need for a new infilling of the Spirit, which found a response in the heart of every one who had spent those ten days waiting upon God. The new setting made to the hymn of Dr. Bonar gave a freshness to it that it might not otherwise have had. At all events the singing of it seemed to harmonize so well with that which was upon the minds and hearts of the people that it was used more than any other hymn, as a duet or solo. I remember particularly how Mr. Moody was impressed with it and how bowed down he became under the spell of the thought emphasized so beautifully by Dr. Bonar.

Following the work of some two months in Detroit, Dr. Pentecost conducted a series of meetings in Chicago in the church that had grown out of Mr. Moody's mission work in that city—the church that came to be known as the "Moody Church."

Noted results came because of that series of meetings in that historic church so greatly owned of God. Meetings held also on the west side of the city, at that period, made them memorable to all who participated.

From Chicago Dr. Pentecost went to Minneapolis, where again the gospel was preached with great power and with blessing to the people in a very unusual way.

With reminiscences of this campaign there always comes the memory of one of the pastors engaged with us. He was not conspicuous as a gifted preacher nor as pastor of one of the prominent churches, but he was known by all as a man whose heart was overflowing with love for everybody. He never spoke to any one without a smile on his face and hardly ever without conveying the impression that the sun was ever shining.

Sometimes a single word becomes associated with a person, which was the case with this good man. I remember that because of his frequent use of the word "sweet," we called him "Sweet William."

I remember also, regarding this friend, that he came into possession of two magnificent greyhounds, one of which had once belonged to that famous Indian fighter, General Custer. He looked upon both animals as all but human, and—how he loved them! Indeed he seemed to feel that they were God's messengers to him.

Many years after this Minneapolis campaign he

wrote me—from his home in California—a letter
whose every line was fragrant with the same spirit
of love that so impressed itself upon all of us that
memorable Spring.

CHAPTER 13

An event that has had much to do with the religious life of this country was the establishing at Northfield, Massachusetts, that following August of the conferences that have made Northfield and its illustrious organizer household words throughout the Christian world.

I recall very well the men who took part in that first conference. Mr. Moody, Major Whittle, Dr. Brooks of St. Louis, Dr. A. J. Gordon of Boston, Dr. Pentecost and Dr. W. J. Erdman. Evangelists George C. Needham, L. W. Munhall and Henry M. Moore of Boston, were among the speakers. Mr. Sankey, Mr. and Mrs. McGranahan, Mrs. Stebbins and myself were among the singers, all of whom have joined the great company of the redeemed on high, save one—besides myself—Dr. Munhall, who is still the Boanerges of the evangel-

98

ists, both in physical strength, intellectual and moral power. That conference, as has been intimated, was characterized by a deep spiritual tone and by the manifest presence of God, and was one that left its mark upon the lives of those attending it.

In the autumn immediately succeeding that conference, Dr. Pentecost conducted two series of meetings, during which he received a call to the pastorate of the Tompkins Avenue Congregational Church of Brooklyn, which he accepted and entered upon at the conclusion of his engagements. This arrangement left Mrs. Stebbins and myself free for the season. Moody and Sankey were then entering upon an all-winter evangelistic campaign in San Francisco, and we were called to that city.

The songs used most by us during that never-to-be-forgotten winter were, "Behold, What Manner of Love," "I Shall Be Satisfied," "Gathering Home," "One by One," "Green Hill" and "Beyond the Smiling and the Weeping." The latter we often sang with Mr. Sankey as a trio, as we also did another impressive hymn of Dr. Bonar's, "Pray, Brethren, Pray—Eternity Is Drawing Nigh," set to music by Philip Phillips.

At the conclusion of that very strenuous winter's work we returned East. At Niagara Falls we received word of President Garfield's assassination, news that came as a thunderbolt to the nation, visibly affecting every one as did the tragedy of the martyred Lincoln.

In the autumn of that year I joined Dr. Pentecost in his work in Brooklyn and established my residence in that city. I assumed direction of the music in his church. In spite of the demands upon him Dr. Pentecost found time to do considerable evangelistic work in other parts of the city and adjacent towns, besides conducting Sunday afternoon services during the winter in the Academy of Music.

The following June, Mr. Moody summoned Dr. Pentecost, Mrs. Stebbins and myself to Scotland to assist him in the closing weeks of their all-winter campaign in Glasgow. On our arrival there we found the city greatly stirred by the evangelistic appeal that had been going out to the multitudes during that winter. Plunging at once into the work of gathering up results, we found our energies taxed by the demands made upon us.

At the close of that work, Mr. Sankey returned to America and Dr. Pentecost went to England

and the Continent, leaving Mrs. Stebbins and myself to assist Mr. Moody in work he had planned
to do in Scotland during the summer. Other cities
had been appealing to him for a campaign; he
therefore arranged to visit several of the larger
places and smaller towns, spending a few days in
the former and a day or two in the latter.

During the great meetings he and Mr. Sankey
held in Edinburgh eight years previously, when
on their first visit to Great Britain, among the
students of the Edinburgh University who came
into the movement was a young man by the name
of Henry Drummond. Mr. Moody soon learned
that this modest and retiring young student had an
extraordinary influence over the young men of the
University, and he at once began using him in
his meetings. There sprang up a very warm
friendship between these two that lasted to the end
of their lives.

Mr. Moody arranged not only for Mrs. Stebbins
and myself to accompany him on his mission that
summer, but included also his friend Drummond.
During a part of the interval that separated their
first meeting in 1873 and this winter's work in
Glasgow Mr. Drummond had been one of the
Professors of the Glasgow University, and had ac-

complished a great work among young men in the
city, as well as in the University, so that his interest in evangelistic work, especially among young
men, had kept him in sympathy with the work
Moody and Sankey had been doing.

It is a pleasure to recall those weeks together.
Mr. Moody, though still preaching two or three
times a day, felt burden-free from the greater
meetings and entered into plans for the summer
much as a tired man does for his summer vacation.

As we traveled from place to place, sometimes
in carriages, he entered into the enjoyment of the
changing scenes as we passed along the roads of
that beautiful country, and into the fellowship of
his delightful companion. The Professor's sharp,
but kindly, eyes saw now and then some interesting specimen in the plant world, which he would
secure and explain to us—he being an authority
in botany. The visits to Aberdeen, Dundee and
other smaller cities and towns were full of interest, as well as fruitful in results. One day we took
a steam yacht and went to Campbelltown (the
home of his friend, the owner of the yacht), which
has long been noted for the manufacture of whisky,
and where it was said that one of the churches
was built very largely from the profits of the sale

of that article in the days when it was considered quite proper for even the ministers to imbibe.

On returning from there Mr. Moody conducted a day's meeting at Paisley, where we were entertained in the castle of Sir Peter Coates—manufacturer of the celebrated Coates thread—situated on the banks of the "Bonnie Doon" which ran through the castle garden.

The last place visited during that delightful summer was Dumfries, the home, at one period of his life, of Robert Burns. After Mr. Moody had conducted the services there for some time, he arranged to leave Professor Drummond, Mrs. Stebbins and myself to continue the meetings while he joined Mrs. Moody in London.

When the few days of meetings we were left to carry on had ended, Mrs. Stebbins and I went on to London and from there to Paris for a short stay before sailing for home, while the Professor made preparation for a trip to Africa on a scientific expedition. Before his departure he took with him to London some lectures he had delivered to the students in the Glasgow University and put them into the hands of a publisher with a view to their publication under the title of "Natural Law in the Spiritual World."

He went on to Africa and immediately buried himself in the very heart of the continent, remaining there some eighteen months. When he finally emerged and was able to get in touch with the world again, he woke to the realization that he was one of the most famous of men, through his book, which had already reached a large sale and was being much discussed in the religious press.

CHAPTER 14

BACK TO LONDON; TABERNACLE CONSTRUCTED OF COR-
RUGATED IRON; MAJOR WHITTLE; JAMES MC GRANA-
HAN; GEORGE WILLIAMS; IN THE ROOM WHERE THE
Y.M.C.A. WAS ORGANIZED; WINDSOR CASTLE; THE "MIL-
ITARY TOURNAMENT"; ROYAL FAMILIES; EARL OF
SHAFTESBURY; LADY AND MISS KINNAIRD; EXETER
HALL; A CHARACTERISTIC OF MOODY; "JERUSALEM";
STRENUOUS DAYS; "BOARDING ROUND"; LADY BEAU-
CHAMP; ADA HABERSHON; HAPPY DAYS ON COUNTRY
ESTATES; MOODY "AT PLAY"; DRUMMOND AND FIRST
CORINTHIANS 13.

The winter following our return from Scotland
was another strenuous season devoted to church
and evangelistic work, much as the winter previous. I found time, however, to do some writing,
and among the several written during that period
are two of my best known hymns—"Jesus Is Calling" and "In the Secret of His Presence."

Of the former there was no incident that occa-
sioned the setting made to Fanny Crosby's words,
"Jesus Is Tenderly Calling," nor did either the
words nor the music impress me as possessing more
than ordinary merit, even for evangelistic work.
The music was written with the view of making

the song available as an invitation hymn; but that it would meet with instant favor, and in a few years would become generally known, did not enter my mind.

I was even more surprised at the reception given to "In the Secret of His Presence," for in making a setting to the beautiful words of a native of East India I thought only of using it as an offertory selection, when a simple song would be desired; hence the rather unusual progressions of harmony that were introduced. The hymn was first used as intended when the setting was made, but afterwards was found suitable for other purposes and gradually came to the attention of singers of sacred songs.

About the time the setting was made—the latter part of 1883—Moody and Sankey began their all-winter mission in London, and as I was in occasional communication with Mr. Sankey, I sent him a manuscript copy of the hymn as a matter of interest rather than with the thought of his singing it. Not long afterward, however, he informed me that he was singing the hymn in their meetings and that it was being well received. He also informed me that one of the daughters of Lady Beauchamp was singing it in London.

The hymn was published in "Gospel Hymns," and in "Songs and Solos," Mr. Sankey's English book. In that way it came to be known on both continents and on the mission fields as well.

A few years later Dr. J. Hudson Taylor, founder of the China Inland Mission, attended one of the summer conferences at Northfield. He said to me one day, "Mr. Stebbins, would you mind writing the music of your hymn 'In the Secret of His Presence' in four part harmony? It is the favorite hymn of our China Inland missionaries, and it is thought that if it were arranged in that manner, instead of with an accompaniment, it would be more convenient for them to sing."

In March of that winter, 1883-84, as already mentioned, I went to London with Dr. Pentecost to assist in the campaign Mr. Moody was conducting.

That all-winter mission was projected upon a large scale, as it was planned to hold services in several of the most strategical locations. In order to accomplish this, and to accommodate the people, corrugated iron tabernacles were constructed and used in various locations, as needed.

In that way the whole city was encircled and the meetings made easily available. Three weeks

were given to each center, and the influence awakened in one being carried to the one following, the
interest was cumulative, and a great wave of blessing passed over the city that made it the most
memorable religious campaign in its history.

The reason for inviting Dr. Pentecost and myself to assist in the movement was because there was
so urgent a demand for meetings in localities too
distant from the great central meetings, and it was
felt important that those demands should be met
so far as possible. For the same reason Major
Whittle and Mr. McGranahan were present during the closing months.

In a great movement of that kind, lasting six
months, amusing as well as touching incidents are
sure to happen, and many interesting people met.
Such proved to be the case that memorable winter.

Of the latter, that which I remember with the
most pleasure was meeting George Williams, the
founder of the Young Men's Christian Association—afterward knighted by Queen Victoria.
Dr. Pentecost and I were invited, immediately on our arrival in London, to his home and
his rare hospitality. I shall not forget the warmth
and cordiality of our reception by that good man,
for unaffected kindness of heart, and an entire

absence of self-consciousness expressed itself in his every movement and word. No face I ever saw radiated a kinder smile or wore a gentler expression—and that not once but always. The many acts of kindness bestowed upon me by that honored man during those weeks, and on other visits to the metropolis, I treasure among my choicest recollections. He took me, at one time, to the large department store of which he was for many years the head, and we entered the very room where the Young Men's Christian Association was organized, and where he told me all about its origin. He was then a young man, and being accustomed to meet employees in that room for prayer (it was also used for a midday lunch room), the thought occurred to him to form an organization for the benefit of the young men associated with him in the store.

I recall a delightful incident that occurred later in the spring. One of his sons, who had been interested in Mr. Moody's work, invited me on a trip to Windsor Castle. Seats were engaged on the top of one of the famous tally-ho coaches, and the ride taken. It was a lovely spring day; the beautiful meadows had on their freshest coat of green, and the foliage along the way was at its best; and as we passed rapidly along it seemed, indeed, as if we were on enchanted ground. The distance was scheduled to be made in three hours, which was very swift traveling behind horses; but three relays of four-horse teams selected for their swiftness made it possible to accomplish the thirty miles in that time.

It was considered quite the thing in those days for an outing, and it was certainly made most delightful and enjoyable. On arrival we were permitted to visit the famous royal castle, which added much to the interest of the day's experiences, especially for an American.

On another occasion the same friend took me to one of the noted annual affairs of London, known as the "Military Tournament," held in one of the great halls capable of seating twenty thousand people, and which had been crowded with men on one or more occasions when Moody and Sankey held meetings there, during their first visit to Great Britain. The occasion of the tournament was the displaying of various military movements and artillery exploits at which some members of the Royal family were to be present. On this occasion the Prince and Princess of Wales—afterward King Edward and Queen Alexandra—were present, and my friend had secured seats near the royal box, hence we had a good opportunity of seeing their highnesses.

The maneuvers of the military and the artillery were both interesting and thrilling to witness, and the affair was enjoyable in the extreme. I asked young Mr. Williams one day why he had taken so much trouble to give me those interesting experiences, and he answered: "When my brother and I took a trip around the world some years ago, our father said to us, 'I want you wherever you are to be as helpful to people you come in contact with as you can,' which we have tried to be."

Another interesting experience occurred in connection with the anniversary exercises of the Young Woman's Christian Association of London that were held that spring. The program as arranged included singing by the Jubilee Singers of America, and an address by the Earl of Shaftesbury, the best known and best loved philanthropist of Great Britain, who was to preside. By request of the Honorable Emily Kinnaird, who was the active head of the Association (though her mother, Lady Kinnaird, was and had been president from its foundation) I assisted in the service, and the combination of talent on the program was interesting, if not amusing.

Miss Kinnaird specially desired me to sing Mr. Bliss's hymn, "Eternity," and though I had a regular engagement in another part of the city, she arranged to bring me to the meeting after the beginning of the service in which I was engaged. I was therefore put on the program with the celebrities mentioned.

The service was held in Exeter Hall, one of the famous halls used for lectures and religious gatherings for many years, and which, at that time, was headquarters of the central branch of the Y.M.C.A. On my arrival I found the hall full to overflowing, with Lord Shaftesbury in the chair. The singing of the Jubilee Singers was, of course, an impressive as well as attractive feature of the meeting, and the address of the great and good man was absorbing in its interest, although his impressive personality attracted my attention closer. He was so much like Lincoln in his stature and build, so much like him in his great heart of sympathy for the poor, and so like him concerned over those in trouble and sorrow, that it was not difficult to place him in the same class with our great Emancipator.

It was Mr. Moody's custom, during that winter, to have an all-day meeting the last day of the series at each center. I recall an incident that occurred at one of those meetings which caused a great deal of amusement. Moody and Sankey, Major Whittle, Mr. McGranahan, Dr. Pentecost and myself had lunched with some friends, and on the way to the afternoon meeting where Major Whittle and Dr. Pentecost were to speak, a remark was made to the latter illustrating one of Mr. Moody's habits of speech that amused him and which found a lodgment in his mind. As Dr. Pentecost arose to speak, Mr. Moody whispered to him: "Pentecost, be short, be short." The doctor began his address by saying, "Mr. Moody has asked me to be short. I notice that he will have three-quarters of an hour of enthusiastic singing in his services, and then he will get up and speak a half hour, but it is not every one that can do that, for any one who can pronounce Jerusalem in two syllables can do almost anything." The remark caused laughter in the congregation and considerable notice by the press of England. Spurgeon's comment upon the incident, or rather upon Mr. Moody's pronunciation of the word, was not only characteristic of that great preacher, but very happy and appropriate. He said: "I thank God there is one man in such hot haste to get the gospel to the people that he does not stop to pronounce all the syllables of every word."

Sundays were very strenuous days with Mr. Moody, and not infrequently with those who assisted him. I remember one of them very well. He called upon me to take Mr. Sankey's place with him and to fill my own appointments also.

The day began with a meeting in the tabernacle at eight o'clock in the morning, followed by one at eleven, others at three in the afternoon and seven in the evening. As each of these services was followed by an inquiry meeting, the day was a very full one. But, as if that were not enough in one day, a service was appointed at an Institute for young men for nine o'clock in the evening, making five services in which Mr. Moody threw himself with all of his wonderful enthusiasm. My duties in those services were to lead the singing for a half hour or more at the beginning and to sing two or three solos. In addition to these five, I had three other meetings in which the same service was required as at the tabernacle. Mr. Moody was in the prime of his manhood, and I, but nine years his junior, was also at the height of my physical endurance, and so far as I recall neither of us was overtired. In those years, however, I never knew Mr. Moody to confess to being tired, so strong was he and so much did he enjoy his work. This was preëminently true of Dr. Pentecost, for he also had an iron constitution and never seemed so happy as in preaching the gospel, which he lived to do till near his eightieth year, dying in the harness while pastor in full charge of Mr. Wanamaker's large church in Philadelphia.

During the closing months of that great mission, I was "boarded round"—as teachers of country schools were entertained in my early days—and fortunate it was for me, whether it was for those teachers or not, for I had the pleasure of coming in touch with the home-life of some members of the nobility, whom I found to be no different from others who were interested in the Lord's work. A notable instance of this was the family of Lady Beauchamp. It was her custom to rent rooms near by where the meetings were held, in each section of the city visited, and, with her son and four daughters, live there for the time being, so as to be near the meetings. The mother and daughters devoted their time and strength to working in the inquiry rooms, taking the names of the inquirers whom they had helped, and, after the meetings, following them up in their homes.

Indeed, I was told that it was the custom of Lady Beauchamp, and had been for years, every Sunday night at midnight to take a cab and go, unattended, to the dance halls of London, trying to induce young women to lead a different life. She was a tall, dignified lady who would attract attention anywhere by her remarkable appearance, and so commanding that she was permitted to come and go at will by proprietors of those places.

Her son, Montague Beauchamp, a Cambridge graduate, became a foreign missionary, and is yet in the field.

I had the pleasure of being entertained for some weeks in the home of Miss Ada Habershon, the author of many beautiful hymns—among which are "Will the Circle Be Unbroken," set to music by Charles H. Gabriel, and "Oh, What a Change!" —the music by Robert Harkness.

Miss Habershon sang with me frequently during those weeks. Up to that time she neither had attempted to write hymns nor to give attention to the special Bible work that in later years brought her into prominence. During the Torrey and Alexander Mission in London Mr. Alexander discov-

ered her ability as a writer of gospel hymns and
arranged with her to write for him exclusively,
which arrangement continued until her death, a
few years prior to his own passing.

At the conclusion of the winter's campaign Mr.
Moody, for himself and a few of his immediate
helpers, accepted invitations from several of his
London friends, who had country estates, to spend
a few days resting and recuperating from the long
and strenuous campaign, away from the crowded
city.

Among friends who accompanied us on those delightful occasions were two of Lord Kinnaird's
daughters, Professor Henry Drummond, and
others.

Mr. Moody enjoyed the relaxation wonderfully
and entered into the social pleasantries with youthful abandon. An occasional service was held in the
various places where we rested for the benefit of
people living thereabout.

Professor Drummond, who was the life of the
party during those days, had a genius for introducing new and novel attractions for the young
people, and possessed a remarkably attractive personality which made him a delightful acquisition
to a company of friends.

I recall with special pleasure one experience we all enjoyed during those warm and sunny days. Mr. Moody got the company seated on the lawn under a large shade tree. After a moment he requested: "Drummond, give us the thirteenth chapter of first Corinthians." The Professor, always reluctant, hesitated, until Mr. Moody insisted that we all wanted to hear his exposition of that pearl of the New Testament. After further persuasion he gave us his delightful reading of the chapter, which in after years was published under the title of "The Greatest Thing in the World," and has become a classic.

CHAPTER 15

In the autumn of 1887 Dr. Pentecost, having
resigned the pastorate of his church in Brooklyn
to devote his entire time to evangelistic work, engaged to conduct a series of meetings in Lawrence,
Massachusetts. While there Mrs. Stebbins and I
were invited to dine with one of the pastors of the
city, who called our attention to the hymn "Throw
Out the Life-line." I was struck at once with the
possibilities of its usefulness and wrote the author
(who was then pastor of a Baptist church on the
coast) asking if he would sell his hymn. He re-

plied that he would and named a satisfactory price, which I paid. As the original music was poorly arranged, I re-harmonized the song, which was published in the next edition of "Gospel Hymns." Before that book was issued, however, it was arranged for male voices and published in "Male Chorus," which Mr. Sankey and I were just then editing. I began singing it very soon and found at once that the song had a mission. It sprang into favor immediately, and from that time on, for many years, was one of the most popular hymns of the kind in use.

The author, Reverend E. S. Ufford, some years later made a tour around the world, singing his song everywhere he went and using it as a text to preach from in arousing Christians to a sense of their obligations to make known the gospel.

In the autumn following, Dr. Pentecost having accepted a call to spend the winter in Scotland, I joined Mr. Moody on the Pacific coast. I remember very well how the hymn got hold of men that winter and how inspiring it was to hear four or five thousand voices singing the chorus.

Mr. Sankey was not with Mr. Moody that winter, and the responsibility of leading the singing, often without adequate support from choirs, fell upon me. This, with much special music required in the various daily meetings, and the intensive work of the inquiry room, proved a severe test of endurance. But the summer's rest, that soon followed those strenuous months, restored wasted energies, and when the fall campaign set in, strength was found equal to the duties imposed.

Mr. Moody had arranged for meetings in several universities of the North, for which Mr. Sankey was not available, and I was called upon to accompany him. After these (in the latter part of the winter) a meeting was planned for New York City, and the services began in the Collegiate Church, Fifth Avenue and Twenty-ninth Street. It was soon found that the church was not large enough to accommodate the people. To meet this emergency it was arranged to have two services each morning—one in the Collegiate Church at 10 o'clock, and the other at the Madison Avenue Presbyterian Church, at Fifty-ninth Street, at 11 o'clock. After conducting the preliminary services at the 10 o'clock meeting, I would go on to the next appointment and keep the people singing until Mr. Moody appeared. As each of these services was followed by an inquiry service, it made the mornings busy.

The afternoons were given to services in the Central branch of the Brooklyn Y.M.C.A., and the evenings were devoted to services in different parts of the city, making, altogether, four services a day—Saturdays excepted. This program was followed for about ten weeks, which made another winter of exacting labors. In none of these meetings had we adequate support from choirs.

To a service in the Collegiate church came a young lady from the West, who was visiting relatives in the city. She had heard of the fame of the evangelist and was desirous of hearing him speak. Mrs. Stebbins and I sang Dr. Doane's beautiful hymn, "Though Your Sins Be As Scarlet," which arrested her attention, she being a singer herself. But as she was not a Christian, the hymn did more than attract her attention. The truth went as an arrow to her heart and conscience and so disturbed her that she hurried away from the meeting as soon as it was out, with the determination not to attend another. The truth, winged by the sweet melody, became so fixed in her mind that she could get no relief, and, instead of being able to keep her resolution, she found herself at the next service, intensely interested in the message of Mr. Moody. Still unhappy and resentful, yet unable to keep away from the meetings, she finally gave up the fight and yielded herself to God's claims upon her. Some time after returning to her home, she became a student at the Moody Bible Institute in Chicago, where I had the pleasure of meeting her during the World's Fair evangelistic campaign which Mr. Moody conducted during the six months of the Fair and during which time she sang with me on occasions. The happy sequel to this story is that she married one of the students of the Institute and went to the foreign field with him, where they have been for many years in mission service.

The song referred to—"Though Your Sins Be As Scarlet"—I discovered in a book published by Bigelow and Main of New York. The book was one that had been succeeded by others and was not at that time in demand. I was impressed with the possible usefulness of the song—if some slight changes were made—in my work. I found various repetitions that seemed unnecessary. These I eliminated and, without materially changing the author's theme, began singing it, as a duet, with Mrs. Stebbins. I found it to be one of the most valuable hymns. Not only because of the attractive melody, but because of the very important truth contained in the words which Fanny Crosby had happily arranged almost wholly from the Scripture. Satisfying myself as to the usefulness of the hymn, as thus arranged, I submitted the changes to Dr. Doane, and he very cordially consented to its use in that form.

Mr. Moody was very fond of the hymn and used it a great deal for many years. It afterward appeared in many gospel hymn books until it became a common favorite and very much blessed wherever used.

The summer following this strenuous winter, Mrs. Stebbins and I accompanied Dr. Pentecost on his visit to India. A campaign among the Europeans connected with the government of that land had been considered.

After the summer conferences at Northfield were over for the season, we set sail for England, and in October, accompanied by the Honorable Gertrude and Emily Kinnaird, who were going in the interest of the Indian Y.M.C.A., we sailed from London direct to Calcutta in the S.S. *Khedive*. There were few matters of interest different from the experiences of other pilgrims over that well-traveled highway. The stopping at coaling stations, where we got a glimpse of native in-

MY REDEEMER

P. P. BLISS

JAMES MCGRANAHAN

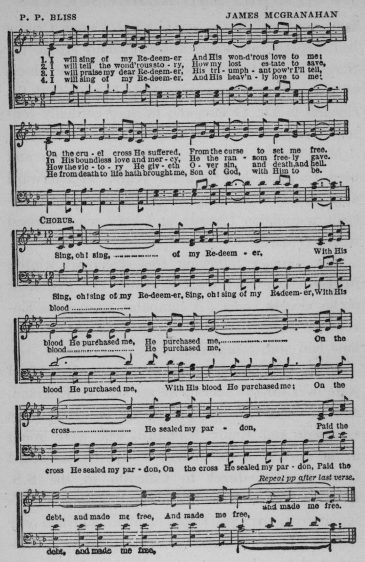

1. I will sing of my Re-deem-er, And His won-d'rous love to me:
2. I will tell the wond'rous sto-ry, How my lost es-tate to save,
3. I will praise my dear Re-deem-er, His tri-umph-ant pow'r I'll tell,
4. I will sing of my Re-deem-er, And His heav'n-ly love to me:

On the cru-el cross He suffered, From the curse to set me free.
In His boundless love and mer-cy, He the ran-som free-ly gave.
How the vic-to-ry He giv-eth O-ver sin, and death, and hell.
He from death to life hath brought me, Son of God, with Him to be.

CHORUS.

Sing, oh! sing, ... of my Re-deem-er, With His
Sing, oh! sing of my Re-deem-er, Sing, oh! sing of my Redeem-er, With His

blood ....
blood He purchased me, He purchased me, ... On the
blood .... He purchased me, With His blood He purchased me; On the

cross .... He sealed my par-don, Paid the
cross He sealed my par-don, On the cross He sealed my par-don, Paid the

Repeat pp after last verse.

and made me free.
debt, and made me free, And made me free,
debt, and made me free,

habitants—their peculiar dress, general appearance and customs; their appeal to you for charity or insistence upon selling their wares, were all interesting to those who saw them for the first time. The day spent at the famous Fortress of Gibraltar, the day at Naples, and the passing through the Red Sea, left the deepest impress upon my mind.

After a day of absorbing interest among the ruins of Pompeii, we sailed out of the far-famed Bay of Naples as the shadows of evening were gathering. The whole Western sky was painted with a brilliancy of color I had never before seen. A stream of fire-red molten lava flowed down the side of Mt. Vesuvius. The entire scene was grand beyond description and left an impress upon my mental vision that time will not destroy. To one who has visualized the passing of the Children of Israel through the Red Sea "on dry land" comes a sense of awe at the greatness and majesty of the God who would so lead His chosen people. And when one realizes that on either side of the sea are the mountains which resounded with the thanksgiving songs of that ancient people, there comes stealing over him the feeling that he is in the very midst of the greatest events in ancient history.

Full of interest was the day spent at Ceylon,

the famous island on the extreme southern point of India. We visited many points of interest; among them the house in which the hymn "From Greenland's Icy Mountains" was written; the cinnamon gardens, etc., finishing our stay with a service at a prominent church. The short stop at Madras, where we held a service in the Y.M.C.A. hall, was also a day of interest and enjoyment.

Preparations for inaugurating the mission in India were made in Calcutta, and shortly after our arrival there (about the middle of November) the work began—the meetings being held in the opera house and attended, very largely, by Europeans.

As the interest developed, Dr. Pentecost, by request, held services for the students of the college, which were largely and enthusiastically attended, although with what result in actual conversions could not be determined, as the young men all belonged to the high castes, the breaking away from which was liable to result in serious consequences. The services, however, served to awaken the educated natives and to secure for Dr. Pentecost a very urgent invitation to conduct similar work among them, which he arranged to do later in the season.

At the conclusion of the series of meetings in

H. R. PALMER

D. L. MOODY

the opera house, the committee in charge of the campaign thought it important that Dr. Pentecost should continue his addresses to the college students. He, accordingly, did so; and as we, quite early in that work, learned that the singing of our special songs served little more than to excite curiosity, it seemed best that Mrs. Stebbins and I should, for the time being, assist the missionaries in their different fields. In carrying out this plan, Bishop Thoburn—the first missionary bishop of the Methodist Episcopal Church in India—who was known and loved among the missionaries of all denominations in that country, arranged for our services and planned our work among them—incidentally making engagements for us to conduct services of song in the principal cities of the empire.

We learned that Miss Goreh, the author of the hymn "In the Secret of His Presence," lived in Allahabad, and, through courtesy of the missionaries of the American Presbyterian Church, had the pleasure of meeting the lady whose hymn had become familiar to many thousands of people on the other side of the world.

I had been told that she was engaged in Christian work among her native sisters; but she was then in attendance upon a sick friend. I found her to be a retiring lady of an attractive and interesting personality, and enjoyed the brief conversation with her greatly. Thus met the writer and the singer—one from the East, the other of the West beyond distant seas—of a song that had carried blessing to untold numbers of God's children.

This plan of visiting the different cities of India afforded us an opportunity not only of seeing much of Indian life among the natives and of the beauty of their architecture, but also of coming into intimate touch with the noble band of missionaries and of seeing the really great work they are accomplishing in that land. It was a great privilege, too, to sow the seeds of the Kingdom by means of sacred song and to have a part in the evangelistic movement of that winter.

One experience we had among the many that will never be effaced from memory was our visit to that pearl of all existing architecture, the Taj Mahal, so justly famed for its unrivaled beauty. One brilliant moonlight evening Mrs. Stebbins and I, accompanied by our son, G. Waring Stebbins, (then a young man in the beginning of his musical career, and a singer, as well, who was assisting in the services of song) visited the place, and while standing immediately under the dome which towered a hundred feet above our heads, we each sounded a note of the common chord and then listened to hear our voices echoed back to us for nearly a minute before the sounds died away in a harmony that seemed heavenly indeed, so pure and free from all imperfection were they and so unlike any other earthly sounds our ears had ever heard.

During the latter part of the season, we had the opportunity of assisting Bishop Thoburn in a short series of meetings in Bombay, and also in Madras; and while engaged in the latter, the first National Y.M.C.A. convention was held there; also the first National Sunday School convention, which gave us the opportunity to sing for them and to conduct the music at their sessions.

At the close of our engagements in Madras, preparations were made for our return to America, and within a fortnight we sailed from Bombay with plans for breaking our journey at Egypt and Palestine en route.

Some time prior to departure, Dr. Pentecost yielded to the urgent request of prominent Brahmin citizens of India to continue his addresses on the historical facts of Christianity and of the fundamental doctrines of the Christian religion, in distinction from the religions of the East. He, therefore, remained for some time to meet those engagements which resulted in his return to India the following season for further work along the same lines and to resume his work among the Europeans connected with the Government.

On our arrival at Ismalia, at the northern end of the Red Sea, some ten days after sailing, we disembarked and took the train for Cairo.

As we passed through the land in which God's ancient people once dwelt, toiled and suffered, and from which they were finally driven by the hand of the oppressor, we came again under the spell of sacred history; and from then on for the days that remained of our stay in the land of the Pharaohs, we were never free from an overpowering sense that we were on the very ground where God had displayed His mighty power and performed His greatest miracles in ancient history.

To say that the seven days spent under those Egyptian skies were absorbing in their interest would be to say what is self-evident, for no one can visit that land without having a bewildered sense of being in another world, seeing unusual sights, hearing strange sounds, and having weird sensations never dreamed of before.

Wandering the streets of the ancient city, visiting the markets and marts of trade, the mosques, the tombs and places where the people congregate; the museum where we looked upon the mummied form and face of the Pharaoh who oppressed the Children of Israel four thousand years before, the face so extraordinarily preserved through four millenniums as to show the remarkable strength that monarch must have possessed; the visit to the ruins of the old city of Memphis, which once had the proud eminence of being the home of the Pharaohs, but now giving little evidence of ever having been anything more than a few stone houses. The visit, riding on donkeys, to the first Pyramid ever constructed; the sight of the tombs of sacred bulls, and other places uncovered after having been buried under the sands of centuries; and later, the visit to the great Pyramids, the climbing to the top, five hundred feet from the ground, of the largest one, which some of the party did, while others went up two hundred and fifty feet into the very heart of it, where a tomb was designed that contained a large granite sarcophagus, in which the great Pharaoh who constructed it had expected his body to rest through the ages, but where no evidence of his remains having been committed to its keeping has ever been discovered —all these produced sensations which would defy the most gifted pen.

The memory of the Sunday spent in that strange city can never be lost. We did not spend any part of the day in sight-seeing, but in the morning attended the Koptic church, the only Christian church there, where we had the great privilege of singing to the praise of God of our salvation, and of Him who came in one of the dark periods of the world's history to redeem mankind. The afternoon of that day was spent in the study of Bible history of God's ancient people—Mrs. Stebbins reading aloud.

When she came to the story of Joseph, our son lay upon the floor, his chin resting in his hands, listening in breathless silence to that most beautiful and fascinating story. It was easy to visualize, under those circumstances, the scenes and tragedies depicted in the life of that great outstanding figure in Biblical history, and as the story unfolded we could all but see its reënactment. So it was with much that we saw in that ancient land of the Pharaohs.

From Egypt we sailed to Palestine, making our first stop at the famous city of Joppa, the nearest place of call for passengers visiting Jerusalem, and as the steamer dropped anchor, a friend, who knew of our coming, came out in a small boat to meet us, quite as much to our pleasure as to our surprise, as we were not expecting him. As we disembarked we, like all passengers, were put into a small boat manned by experienced and sturdy men with oars, who very skillfully took us through the narrow passageway between rocks that have stood guard at the entrance of that harbor for centuries, and delivered us safely on the shores of that sacred land.

We proceeded by stage to Jerusalem, where we were met at the Joppa gate by Mrs. Spafford of the American Colony, whom we had known in Chicago, and who made us very comfortable during our stay in the city.

There we found Dr. and Mrs. H. R. Palmer, and also our very warm friend, Mr. R. C. Morgan, editor of the London *Christian,* who traveled with us through Palestine after completing our visit in the city most sacred to Christians the world over. Dr. and Mrs. Palmer preceded us to other parts of the country.

During the days of our stay there, we visited the principal places of interest in and about the city, being conducted by a member of the Colony who was intimately acquainted with the city.

We had the great privilege of singing there and of giving a service of song also, which we looked upon as one of the outstanding experiences of our lives. The first song I sang was "There Is a Green Hill Far Away," which I was privileged to do in sight and sound of the place where the world's greatest tragedy was enacted.

Aside from the opportunity of visiting the places made forever sacred by the footsteps of our Lord, there is one other experience that will remain with me, and that was our visit to the Mount of Olives.

A company of us took lanterns one moonlight night—which every one was obliged to do when going through the city—as there were no street lights in those days—and wended our way out through the gate, through the Garden of Geth-semane, up the slopes of the Mount and there sat down to view the city from that famous mountain-side.

As we sat silently viewing the city of so many sacred memories, we saw others, like ourselves, coming out of the gate of the city with lanterns

as did the soldiers nineteen hundred years before
to arrest the Savior and take Him to the Judgment
Hall to be condemned as a malefactor. We visualized the rabble that thronged His way to the cross
where He made expiation for the sins of the world
—even for those who were guilty of His death—
and it required little imagination to reënact that
scene in the tragedy, for we were under the same
sky and on the same mountainside. While thus
our thoughts were recalling that saddest of all
the world's events, one of the party began singing
the hymn, " 'Tis midnight, and on Olive's brow,"
in which we all joined with a sense of reality most
solemn and impressive.

After visiting the places of greatest interest in
and about Jerusalem, including Bethlehem and
Bethany, we journeyed by sea to northern Palestine, going from Haifa, where we disembarked, to
Nazareth by stage, across the plains of Esdraelon,
and from Nazareth to Tiberias, on the shores of
Galilee, by horse and donkey, as the wagon road
over that stretch of eight or ten miles was bad.

There were few points of interest to take our
attention in or about Nazareth, aside from Mary's
Well, which was said to be the identical one from
which the mother of our Lord frequently drew

water, as all the inhabitants of that city have been
wont to do throughout all the centuries gone by,
hence its name. We drank of its cooling water,
and thought of the years when Mary's Son did
likewise, as He, like other men, earned His bread
by the sweat of His brow.

We also gazed upon the hills about the city,
as He must have many times rested His weary
eyes upon the beauty of the landscape. We tried
to think of Him at His carpenter's bench; of His
going in and out among His townsmen; of His
assuming His share of the burdens of the family
and His share of the responsibilities of the government of the city; of His living the simple life of
the community, ennobling toil by setting an example to all who should follow Him in the common walks of life; of His loyalty to a perfect
standard of righteousness, and to the principles of
the Golden Rule He afterwards established as the
perfect rule of life.

We were privileged to sing our songs in Nazareth, as we remained there over the Sabbath. Arrangements were made for a service as in other
places, and we counted it one of the most impressive experiences of our lives.

It is needless to say that our visit to Tiberias

was most absorbing in its interest. Memories of scenes that were enacted and of the marvelous works wrought on the shores and upon the turbulent waters of that sacred sea, came trooping from the past to assure us that we were on the very ground where some of the mightiest acts of God had been witnessed. And what a privilege it was to look out upon the blue waters of that sea and wander along its shores.

Our stay in that enchanted place was prolonged beyond our expectation because of a temporary illness of one of the party, which gave us the opportunity of singing in a special service arranged for us and of assisting in a medical mission in the city. We were surprised by the physcan in charge telling us that he had heard Mrs. Stebbins and myself sing in Glasgow a number of years before, naming the hymn we sang that impressed him most, which was Mr. Ogden's beautiful hymn "Gathering Home." A similar remark was made to me on the streets of one of the cities of India by a gentleman who stopped and asked if my name was Stebbins; when I told him it was, he remarked that he heard me sing the same song in Glasgow years before, and it had impressed him so that he remembered it to that day. These incidents gave us the feeling that the world was not so very large after all.

The last songs we sang in that land of sacred lore was in Haifa, before embarking for Italy, in a mission conducted by German missionaries.

As that port of call lay at the foot of Mount Carmel, whereon God had wrought such wondrous miracles through His servant Elijah, we were privileged to stand upon its summit, to look out upon the great sea, and amid those impressive surroundings to recall God's wonderful dealing with the true and the false prophets.

During our weeks of stay in Egypt and Palestine, so strange and ancient everything appeared that we seemed to have been suddenly taken back two thousand years, and were living the events of those far-off days. When, therefore, the shores of that land faded from our view, as we sailed homeward bound, we awoke to realize we were once more under modern skies, and would ere long be in the midst of modern life in the new world beyond the seas.

As a brief visit to the Continent was scheduled in the plans for our homeward journey, it was arranged by friends that we should give services of song in three of the cities of Italy, beginning with Naples.

This was held in the Presbyterian church; the next in the Methodist and Presbyterian missions in Rome, and the third in the Presbyterian church in Florence.

We counted it an honor to be permitted to sing our message of salvation in that land of song, and a privilege to visit those cities crowded with so much of intense interest relating not only to ancient history, but to modern life. To visit the galleries and look upon the famous works of modern and ancient art was an experience of a lifetime, and a pleasure no words can describe.

A brief visit to Venice, that pearl of Italian cities, a few days gazing upon the beauty and grandeur of the Swiss lakes and mountains, a few days in Paris, with a service of song in the American church, and a few days' rest in London preparatory to sailing for home brought us to the end of our mission to the Far East.

CHAPTER 16

The year following our return from India—from the summer of 1891 to the autumn of 1892—nothing occurred worthy of mention here; but in October of the latter year Mr. Moody cabled me to join him in Great Britain for a work that had been planned the winter he and Sankey spent in Scotland. After our work in several of the principal cities of England, we went to London for a

142

campaign in Spurgeon's Tabernacle. On our arrival in that city Mr. Moody became anxious concerning a severe cold which had settled in his throat and interfered greatly with his speaking. I prevailed upon him to call Dr. Habershon, who discovered an irregular heart action. He assured us there was no occasion for immediate anxiety, but warned the patient against excessive work.

Before the doctor left, he got Mr. Moody's consent to make an appointment with Sir Andrew Clark, then the most famous physician in London, for expert advice. The appointment was made for a day immediately at the close of the services in the Tabernacle and following a banquet given Mr. Moody by his London friends, which was presided over by George Williams.

At Sir Andrew's examination of Mr. Moody he assured us that Dr. Habershon had made a correct diagnosis, and endorsed the advice the young physician had given. During his examination, Sir Andrew asked Mr. Moody, whom he knew by reputation, how often he preached. "Three times a day, usually," replied Mr. Moody, "sometimes four —except one day I reserve for rest." After a moment of silence the doctor asked: "What kind of a man are you, anyway?" Mr. Moody came back with the inquiry: "Sir Andrew, how many hours a day do you work?" When told "fifteen to eighteen," Mr. Moody retorted with, "What kind of a man are you, anyway?" He was advised to limit his preaching to one or two services a day, to be careful about overexerting himself and to exercise judgment as to his diet. This Mr. Moody promised to do, and from that time more carefully restricted himself in his public activities.

From London we went to Dublin for a fortnight's mission, which was held in a large hall, sometimes used for a rink.

Soon after the close of these engagements, which proved to be his last work in Great Britain, he sailed with his son, William R. Moody, for New York on the S. S. *Spree* of the North German Lloyd. When about a thousand miles from Queenstown, the shaft of the steamer broke and a rush of water into some of the stern compartments caused the ship to settle at that end. Being a single screw steamer, she was left at the mercy of the sea.

Among the passengers was General O. O. Howard, at that time Commandant of the Army of the East with headquarters at Governor's Island. He was known not only for his great service to his country, but for being an outstanding

Christian man and actively interested in all forms of aggressive Christian work.

As he and Mr. Moody were long-time friends, they often met, no doubt for prayer, in that time of fear lest the great ship with its large list of passengers should founder.

It was said that both of these men were constantly busy encouraging as best they could the frightened people, and that Mr. Moody spoke to them in a body, making use of the most encouraging portions of Scripture.

The following account of that experience, given by Mr. Moody himself, is taken from a biography, written by his son, W. R. Moody:

"When about three days out on our voyage, I remember I was lying on my couch, as I generally do at sea, congratulating myself on my good fortune, and feeling very thankful to God. I considered myself a very fortunate man, for in all my travels by land and sea I had never been in an accident of a serious nature.

"While engaged with these grateful thoughts, I was startled by a terrible crash and shock, as if the vessel had been driven on a rock. I did not at first feel much anxiety—perhaps I was too ill to think about it. My son jumped from his berth and rushed on deck. He was back again in a few moments, exclaiming that the shaft was broken and the vessel sinking. I did not then think it could be so bad, but concluded to dress and go on deck. The report was only too true. The ship's passengers were naturally aroused, but in answer to frightened inquiries they were assured it was only a broken shaft.

"The serious nature of the accident soon became evident, however, as other passengers rushed on deck declaring their cabins were filling with water. Later it was found that the two fractured ends of the shaft, in revolving, had broken the stern tube, admitting water into two after-most compartments, which were immediately filled. The bulkhead between the compartments was closed at once and braced with beams to resist the pressure of the water. For two days the ship drifted in this helpless condition, in momentary peril from the tremendous beating force of the water in the flooded compartments, as the ship rolled. But for the skill of Captain Willigerod and his efficient engineers, Messrs. Meissel and Baum, the ship would soon have foundered.

"The officers and crew did all they could to save the vessel. But it was soon found that the pumps were useless, for the water poured into the ship too rapidly to be controlled. There was nothing more in the power of man to do, and the ship was absolutely helpless, while the passengers could only stand still on the poor drifting, sinking ship and look into possible watery graves.

"All this time, unknown to the passengers, the officers were making preparations for the last resort. The life-boats were put in readiness, provisions were prepared, life preservers were brought out, the officers were armed with revolvers to enforce their orders, and it was only a question of whether to launch the boats at once or wait. The sea was so heavy that the boats could hardly have lived in it.

"At noon the captain told the passengers that he had the water under control and was in hopes of drifting in the way of some passing steamer. The ship's bow was now high in the air, while the stern seemed to settle more and more. The sea was rough, and the ship rolled from side to side, lurching fearfully. The captain tried to keep up hope by telling the anxious people that they would probably drift in the way of a ship by three o'clock that afternoon, but the night closed in upon us without the sign of a sail.

"That was an awful night—several hundred men, women and children, waiting for the doom that seemed to be settling upon us! No one dared to sleep. We were all together in the saloon of the first cabin—Jews, Protestants, Catholics and skeptics—although I doubt if at that time there were many skeptics among us. The agony and suspense were too great for words. With blanched faces and trembling hearts the passengers looked at one another as if trying to read in the faces of each other what no one dared to speak. Rockets flamed into the sky, but there was no answer. We were drifting out of the track of the great steamers, and every hour seemed to increase the danger of our situation.

"Sunday dawned without help or hope. Up to that time no suggestion for religious services had been made. To have done that would almost certainly have produced a panic. In the awful suspense and dread that prevailed, a word about religion would have suggested the most terrible things to the passengers. It was necessary to divert their minds, if possible, or they would break under the strain. But as that second night came on, I asked General O. O. Howard, who was with us, to secure the captain's consent for a service in the saloon. The captain said: 'Most certainly; I am that kind too.' We gave notice of the meeting and, to our surprise, almost every passenger attended, and I think everybody prayed, skeptics and all.

"With one arm clasping the pillar to steady myself on the reeling vessel, I tried to read the 91st Psalm, and we prayed that God would still the raging of the sea and bring us to our desired haven. It was a new psalm to me from that hour. The eleventh verse touched me very deeply. It was like a voice of divine assurance, and it seemed a very real thing as I read: 'He shall give his angels charge over thee, to keep thee in all thy ways.' Surely He did it! I read also from the 107th Psalm, 20-31. One lady thought those words must have been written for the occasion and afterwards asked to see the book for herself. A German translated it verse by verse as I read it, for the benefit of his countrymen.

"I was passing through a new experience. I had thought myself superior to death. I had often preached on the subject and urged Christians to realize the victory. During the Civil War I had been under fire without fear. I was in Chicago during the great cholera epidemic, and went around with the doctors visiting the sick and dying; where they could go to look after the bodies of men, I said I could go to look after their souls. I remember a case of smallpox where the sufferer's condition was beyond description, yet I went to the bedside of that poor sufferer again and again, with Bible and prayer, for Jesus' sake. In all this I had no fear of death.

"But on the sinking ship it was different. There was no cloud between me and my Savior. I knew my sins had been put away, and if I died it would only be to wake up in heaven. That was settled long ago. But as my thoughts went out to my loved ones at home—my wife, my children, my friends on both sides the sea, the schools and all the interests dear to me—and as I realized that perhaps the next hour would separate me forever from all these, so far as this world was concerned, I confess I almost broke down. It was the darkest hour of my life.

"I could not endure it, I must have relief, and relief came in prayer. God heard my cry, and enabled me to say, from the depth of my soul, 'Thy will be done!' Sweet peace came to my heart. Let it be Northfield or heaven, it made no difference now. I went to bed, fell asleep almost immediately, and never slept more soundly in my life.

"Out of the depth I cried unto the Lord and He heard me and delivered me from all my fears. I can no more doubt that God gave answer to my prayer for relief than I can doubt my own existence.

"About three o'clock in the morning I was aroused from my sound sleep by my son's voice: 'Come on deck, father,' he said. I followed him and found every one eagerly watching a far-off light rising and sinking on the sea. It was a messenger of deliverance to us. It proved to be the light of the steamer *Lake Huron*, bound from Montreal to Liverpool, whose lookout had seen our signal of distress and supposed it was a vessel in flames. Oh, the joy of that moment when these seven hundred passengers beheld the approaching ship! Who can ever forget it!

"But now the question was, 'Can this small steamer tow the helpless *Spree* a thousand miles to Queenstown?' Every moment was passed in intense anxiety and prayer. It was a brave and perilous undertaking. The vessels were at last connected by two great cables. If a storm arose these cables would snap like thread, and we must be left to our fate. But I had no fear. God would finish what He had begun. The waves were calmed, the cables held, our steamer moved in the wake of the *Lake Huron*. There were storms all about us, but they came not nigh our broken ship. Seven days after the accident, by the good hand of God upon us, we were able to hold a joyous thanksgiving service in the harbor of Queenstown. The rescuing ship that God sent to us in our distress had just sufficient power to tow our steamer, and just enough coal to take her into port. Her captain was a man of prayer. He besought God's help to enable them to accomplish their dangerous and difficult task; and God answered the united prayers of the distressed voyagers and brought us to our desired haven."

At the close of Mr. Moody's mission in Dublin, just prior to his sailing for America, I joined Major Whittle, who had been engaged for a short time in evangelistic work in some of the smaller cities of Ireland. The Evangelistic Committee of Dublin had planned a campaign in the small towns of the country, with a view to reach the people of outlying districts who were cut off from privileges the people of the cities enjoyed.

It was an interesting experience, the months we spent among the warm-hearted people of the coun-

try towns, though void of anything of a spectacular nature. The eagerness with which they listened
to the simple gospel of the grace of God, and the
anxiety that many of them manifested to secure
a copy of the New Testament, which was given to
all who desired one, was very heartening and refreshing.

It was not the design of the Dublin Committee
to proselyte, nor would the Major have willingly
lent himself to that, but rather to get the word of
God into the hearts and hands of the people, believing most devoutly that it was the will of God.

There was deep interest everywhere manifested,
and many conversions, but the amount of good accomplished can be revealed only by the records that
are kept on high.

The last meetings of that busy winter were in
Belfast, where great blessings were received during the weeks we labored. The churches were all
heartily united and a widespread spirit of inquiry
was awakened among the people.

Major Whittle's daughter, May, whose beautiful
music set to many of her father's hymns has become
familiar to all lovers of gospel hymns, was with
us during that winter and contributed greatly to
the blessing in the meetings by her singing and her

work among the young women in the towns visited. As Mrs. Stebbins was unable to be with me that winter, I was most happy to avail myself of her assistance in the rendering of many of the special selections. She possessed a voice of rare sweetness and richness of quality, that had been well trained in the Royal Academy of London.

At Christmas time a few days of rest were given us, a portion of which I spent with a friend in Glasgow. Dr. Andrew Bonar had been for many years the pastor of a church in that city, and, desiring to hear him again (having had that pleasure many times at Northfield), I attended his Sunday morning service and listened to an impressive Christmas sermon. Although past eighty-five years of age, he was still in possession of his mental powers, unimpaired by the duties of a strenuous life.

The next day my friend and I called upon the Doctor at his home, where we spent an hour in delightful fellowship with him, and where at the close of our visit he gave us his blessing, which has ever seemed like a benediction from the very Throne itself, so near did he always seem to his Lord.

When I called again two or three days later, his

daughter met me at the door and said her father was not well, and that it would not be well for him to receive friends.

I left my good-by and love for him and went on to continue the work with Major Whittle in Ireland. The next day a dispatch came from his home which announced that he had passed into the presence of his Lord whom he had served so loyally all his long life. The beautiful Christmas sermon I had the privilege of hearing that Sunday morning proved to be his last message to his people and to the land he loved.

Dr. Bonar had many years been recognized as one of the most saintly men of Scotland, and one of its most distinguished Bible scholars. He well deserved and shared the fame of his brother Horatio, the poet, who was also a preacher of great fame and power.

Those who were present at the two Northfield conferences which Dr. Bonar attended—1882 and in 1885—will never forget the blessing he brought to them, not only by his masterly exposition of the Word, but by his very presence. I recall an incident that occurred in 1880. He had been speaking most impressively daily for some time, and with great blessing to the people, when Mr. Moody said to him: "Dr. Bonar, I want you to tell us how it is that you have been able to live the life you have been describing to us." The Doctor shook his head as a smile radiated his saintly face; but Mr. Moody said to him again: "But, Dr. Bonar, the people have been listening from day to day to your messages and they want to know the secret of the life you have been describing." Again the Doctor shook his head, and again that smile as a reflection from another world illumined his countenance. Mr. Moody, with his usual insistence on having his own way in such matters, persisted in his demand. At last Dr. Bonar arose and said: "Brethren, I don't like to speak of myself, but for fifty years I have had daily access to the throne of grace," and with those words, spoken in the most simple manner, took his seat. He could not have said more had he spent the whole morning in explaining the pathway that led him into the secret of a victorious life.

Before his return to Scotland on his second visit to Northfield, I had the honor of entertaining him in my home in Brooklyn. And while there, he expressed the desire to visit West Point. I arranged to escort him to that famous place, and on the appointed day we took one of the beautiful day line steamers on the Hudson, which was an added pleasure to him. Arriving at the celebrated military academy, I took him at once to General O. O. Howard, who spared no pains to make our visit pleasant and interesting.

Major Whittle was on the staff of General Howard during the later years of the war, and from the pulpit often spoke affectionately of his General. Not infrequently the Commander attended our services, and the Major always insisted that he speak to the people. It was through this channel, as well as at conventions, that I met and became acquainted with General Howard.

As a key to the simple and childlike faith that great man ever manifested in his attitude toward God, I once heard him say that in former times when some one jostled him in a crowd or struck his armless shoulder (which was always tender), he used to express some impatience, until one day he decided that a much better plan would be to *pray* for the person who had in that way caused him pain; and ever since that time, he said, instead of complaining he had prayed.

Another feature in the life of the General that impressed me greatly, was the heroic deed he performed among the Indians in the West, when he had been sent, by the Government, to put down the uprising among them, which other officers of the army had failed to accomplish.

The Government had been trying to capture the famous chief, Geronimo, or cause him to surrender; but they had failed in every effort. When General Howard took command of the expedition, he said to his staff, "I am going into the Indian Chief's camp. Is there any one of you who will volunteer to accompany me?" Of course there was a response, and, taking one of his officers, they made their way, unarmed, to the camp. The Chief, who was surprised at the approach of the officers without gun or sword, admitted them into his presence and listened to what the General had to say, who assured him they had not come to do him injury, but to induce him to surrender to the Government.

The Chief was so impressed by the bravery of the General that he bade him retire to one of the tents, and in the morning he would make known his decision. This the officers did, and in the morning the Chief surrendered.

In the spring of 1893, at the conclusion of our work on the other side, I hastened home, because of sickness in my family, the Major and daughter coming later. On their arrival in New York, they went to spend a day or two with General Howard, who was then stationed on Governor's Island.

Sometime prior to the inauguration of the World's Fair Exposition in 1893, Mr. Moody planned to conduct an evangelistic campaign in Chicago to continue through the duration of the fair, being impressed with the opportunity it would afford to reach many thousands of people who would be visiting the city during that period.

To accomplish this, he arranged to have simultaneous meetings every night in various parts of the city.

With this in view he secured several of the most prominent evangelists in this country and from abroad, with as many singers and leaders of singing as were needed; then selected the most strategic points in the city where meetings could be held either in churches, halls or tents erected for the purpose.

Many services were held in theaters on Sundays, and when Forepaugh's circus came to town the great tent was placed at Mr. Moody's disposal on Sunday, without charge. Hence every available place that was thought desirable for conducting a meeting was secured during that long campaign.

The planning for the daily meetings, speaking

on an average once a day, the listening to reports from each of the centers at the close of each day, added to the raising of money to carry it on, taxed the strength and resourcefulness of even so strong a man as Mr. Moody. However, he proved equal to the task, tired though he was when the day's work was done.

It was his custom to hear reports of the meetings that had been conducted by the evangelists as they came in from their various engagements at night and to have refreshments served them in his office in the Bible Institute, where they and their singers were entertained.

At such times, feeling the need of something to take the strain from his mind, he would often say to one of the evangelists noted for being always ready with some amusing incident or story: "W—, give us a story." The request would no sooner be made than the story was forthcoming, and no one would laugh more heartily than Mr. Moody himself. The telling of his story would often suggest one from another of the company, and that, in turn, enthuse some one else, to the enjoyment and relaxation of all.

Thus, after a brief prayer, the day would close and all retire to needed rest.

Each day began with some special singing by soloists and by a chorus of men, followed by an address before the students of the Bible Institute by some one of the evangelists or noted men who happened to be visiting there at the time, which was looked upon as an auspicious beginning of the day's work as then and there outlined.

Many interesting incidents occurred during those busy days. During one of the services Mr. Moody was conducting in Forepaugh's circus tent one Sunday afternoon, a little girl strayed from her mother and got lost in the great crowd of fifteen or twenty thousand people, the most of whom were standing. Some one, seeing the frantic child, took her and carried her to Mr. Moody and told him she was lost. Taking her in his arms he held her up before the great throng and cried at the top of his voice, "A lost child! A lost child!" The anxious mother, seeing her in the great man's arms, rushed up to receive her babe. Mr. Moody, as by an inspiration, made use of the incident in his graphic way to impress upon the minds of the careless and indifferent their lost condition before God, and the fact that the Savior was there even then seeking to find and to save.

That ever-to-be-remembered campaign was of

such a nature that the results could not well be tabulated, even if Mr. Moody had been disposed to keep a record of them, which was never his custom to do in his evangelistic work, believing, as he did, that if he was faithful in proclaiming the truth God would take care of the results.

If the burden of that long campaign, that was never lifted for one wakeful hour from the shoulders of the evangelist, made any inroads upon his vitality, either physical or mental, it was not evident to his friends. It certainly was not manifest in any lessening of his energy or enthusiasm for the salvation of men.

In the light of warning given him by the London physicians the autumn before, however, it would not be wide of the mark to conclude that the long unremitting strain did undermine, to some extent, his vital force. In any event, during the few years that remained of his eventful life, it was very evident to all his friends that he was becoming conscious of his limitations, and that his former great strength and animation were not to be depended upon as in the years when there seemed to be no limit to his physical ability.

In my own case I realized more in after years than at the time, that the use of my voice in leading the singing with poor support at best, in congregations never the same and made up of people from every part of the land who were not familiar with the hymns, made a supreme test of endurance, both of my voice and vitality.

From the beginning of my public activities in the evangelistic field I was not always situated so I could save my voice, hence there were demands upon it that rendered the preservation of the finer qualities difficult, if not impossible. Yet there seemed no alternative; it was therefore used regardless of the injuries that might result—an experience more or less true with all the earlier evangelistic singers.

The plan adopted in later years of having a leader to devote all his energies in directing the choir and congregation, and a singer to do little else than the solo work—a custom inaugurated, or at least greatly emphasized—by Mr. Alexander, seems a wise one.

My contemporaries, as well as myself, however, were both leaders and soloists, which may explain, in part at least, the early breaking down of Mr. McGranahan, and Mr. Sankey, for neither had reached the allotted span of life when they were laid aside from all public activities.

At the close of this strenuous campaign I returned to evangelistic work among the churches, giving the most of my time for the three ensuing years to assisting Major Whittle.

During the August Conference at Northfield in 1893, Fanny Crosby, who was a guest in Mr. Sankey's summer home, was invited to address the conference at one of its sessions. At the close of her remarks she quoted the verses of "Saved by Grace"—a hymn that has become one of her most famous and best loved.

That evening Mr. Sankey asked: "Fanny, where did you get the hymn you quoted at the close of your address to-day?" She replied, with a smile, that she had stored it away in her memory, to use when she was asked to address meetings, and added, "I don't intend to let any of you singers have it, either," meaning thereby that she did not want it set to music, lest it become well known and less desirable for her individual use. "That's right, Fanny, don't you let anybody have it," replied Sankey.

But providentially, it would seem, a representative of the "London Christian" heard her speak, and not knowing of her desire to keep the poem

SAVED BY GRACE

FANNY J. CROSBY

GEO. C. STEBBINS

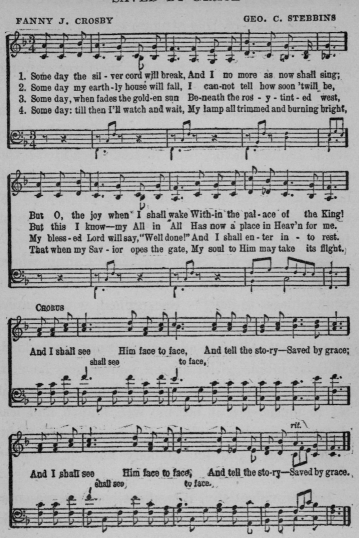

1. Some day the sil - ver cord will break, And I no more as now shall sing;
2. Some day my earth - ly house will fall, I can - not tell how soon 'twill be,
3. Some day, when fades the gold - en sun Be - neath the ros - y - tint - ed west,
4. Some day: till then I'll watch and wait, My lamp all trimmed and burning bright,

But O, the joy when I shall wake With - in the pal - ace of the King!
But this I know—my All in All Has now a place in Heav'n for me.
My bless - ed Lord will say, "Well done!" And I shall en - ter in - to rest.
That when my Sav - ior opes the gate, My soul to Him may take its flight.

CHORUS

And I shall see Him face to face, And tell the sto - ry—Saved by grace;
shall see to face,

And I shall see Him face to face, And tell the sto - ry—Saved by grace.
shall see to face.

rit.

exclusive, he took the verses in shorthand, with her address, and in a few weeks published them.

One day in the early fall, Mr. Sankey came to my house and said to me, "George, do you remember the hymn Fanny quoted in Northfield which she wanted to keep for her own use? Here it is in the 'Christian,' and since it is published, I think it better be set to music. Suppose you try and see what you can do."

Not long after this he and Mr. Moody were holding a series of meetings in Providence, R. I., at the same time Major Whittle and I were engaged in Newport. It was at that time Fanny's Crosby's beautiful hymn was given its musical setting.

Before his meetings closed in Providence, Mr. Moody came down to Newport to address our meeting, and I was prompted to start the new song on its mission at that time. Accordingly Mrs. Stebbins and I sang it for the first time to the great throng which had come to hear Mr. Moody.

The song, and especially the chorus in which occurs the words, "Saved by Grace," evidently impressed him, for at the conferences at Northfield the next summer, Mr. Moody had us sing it two and three times a day. One of his famous sermons was upon the subject of Grace—a subject he loved very much—which was doubtless responsible for his using the hymn as much as he did, not only at that time, but in his work in after years.

As a striking manner in which the hymn has been made a blessing, I mention an incident that occurred some years after its publication, the account of which was given in a Pennsylvania newspaper:

"The congregation of Christ Episcopal Church was startled yesterday morning by a sensational supplement to the morning service. The church was well filled, and devout worshipers responded to the service. The reading had been concluded, and the rector was about to make the usual announcements, when an incident occurred such as old Christ Church never dreamed of. Out of the usual line in a church of this denomination, it was nevertheless marked in its effect and will never be forgotten by those present.

"In the fourth pew from the front aisle of the church sat a neatly-dressed woman of intellectual face, apparently about thirty years of age. Her presence as a stranger had been noticed by many, and her deep, tearful interest had been quietly commented upon by those occupying adjoining pews. At the point mentioned, she rose to her feet and, struggling with emotion, began to speak. The startled congregation was all attention, as she was allowed to proceed.

"Rapidly and eloquently she told of her going out from the church and of her return to it. In graphic words she painted the hideousness of sin, and of the joys of a pure life, and as she spoke men and women gave way to their emotions and listened breathlessly to the end of the narration.

"'I was christened in this church,' she said, 'and attended the Sunday school in the basement when Dr. Paige was rector. My mother was a devout member here and taught me the right way. At the age of fifteen I deserted my home and married an actor. For a number of years I followed the profession, leading such a life as naturally accompanies it. In dramatic circles, in variety, business, and in the circus, I spent those godless years.

"'About two years ago I was in the city of Chicago, and one afternoon was on my way to a park to spend the afternoon in revelry, when I happened on an open air meeting which the Epworth League of Grace Methodist Episcopal Church was conducting on North Clark Street. I stopped through curiosity, as I believed, to listen; but I know now that God arrested my footsteps there. They were singing, 'Saved by Grace,' and the melody attracted me. Recollections of my childhood days came trooping into my soul, and I remembered that in all the years of my absence my mother, until her death, nine years ago, had been praying for me.

" 'I was converted, and, falling on my knees on the curbstone, I asked the Father's pardon. Then and there I received it, and I left the place with a peace that has never forsaken me. I gave up my business and have lived for His service ever since. Last night I visited Hope Mission, and the Lord told me I must come here and testify what He has done for me. I have not been in this building for many years, but it seems only yesterday that I left it. I have been sitting in the pew directly opposite the one once occupied by my mother and myself, and I feel her presence to-day. I could not resist the impulse to give this testimony. The Lord sent me here.'

"The congregation was profoundly impressed; the rector descended the chancel and, approaching the speaker, bade her Goodspeed. The service went on, and at its conclusion many shook hands

with the stranger.   One might have imagined himself in a Methodist Episcopal Church, so intense
was the feeling.   The visitor departed with a sense
of a duty done.   All she said was: 'I feel that the
Lord Jesus and my mother are here.' "

There were four events in those days that stand
out in memory like milestones on one's journey—
the Ecumenical Foreign Missionary Conference
held in Carnegie Hall, New York, in 1900, the
Christian Endeavor Convention held in Madison
Square Garden in 1892, the Fiftieth Anniversary
of the Founding of the Y. M. C. A. in America,
held in Boston in 1893, and the Second Christian
Endeavor Convention held in Boston in 1895.

The event of 1900 was an international affair,
delegates from the various Protestant evangelical
denominations of the world were present, among
whom were many notable men who had come together to confer on the best method of advancing
the cause of Christianity among the uncivilized peo-
ples of the earth, and of the advisability and prac-
ticability of the different agencies coöperating in
their efforts.   It was considered the most important
gathering ever held for the purpose.

The conference was presided over by Ex-Presi-
dent Harrison, who delivered the most eloquent

address, in many respects, that was heard there. Many celebrated men from our own, and from foreign countries, were among the speakers and in attendance upon the sessions.

William McKinley and Theodore Roosevelt—then Governor of New York State—were among those who made addresses and who added great interest to the occasion. One of the brilliant speeches made during those interesting days was delivered by a woman who was prominent in the work at that time, but who has since become known throughout the foreign missionary world, as one of the most able advocates of the missionary cause. I refer to Mrs. Helen Montgomery of Rochester, New York.

Her address was appealing to a remarkable degree, while her attractive personality, her unaffected manner and grace of speech, made her address one to be remembered as among the most impressive delivered during the conference.

As the singing was under my direction, I had the rare privilege of seeing and of hearing many of the most notable people identified with the Foreign Missionary movements of the world, which has ever been one of my most delightful recollections of those by-gone years.

The Christian Endeavor Convention was the largest delegated gathering in the history of the Society up to that time—there being thirty thousand registered. And that which made the occasion impressive in the extreme was the presence of eighteen thousand people in the great auditorium from day to day, and the sound of their voices as they joined in singing their militant songs.

The organizing of the choir of two thousand singers to assist in leading the services of song, and the conduct of the singing during the convention was placed in my hands. Mr. Sankey assisted by singing special selections which added greatly to the musical features of the sessions.

Among the speakers, besides Dr. Clark, the founder of the Society, were Whitelaw Reid, Ambassador to Great Britain, Chauncey Depew, and other celebrated men from our country and from abroad.

As that great hall was not large enough by nearly one-half to accommodate the delegates, not to mention the thousands of visitors desiring to attend the services, simultaneous meetings were held in halls and churches made available for the purpose, where the same programs were carried out as nearly as possible, so that all could have the privilege of enjoying the events of those crowded days.

This great outpouring of the young people of the land engaged in the common cause of service for the kingdom of God was a striking illustration of the growing power and influence of the organization, and seemed at that time the culmination of its years of effort to utilize the youth of the churches.

The Christian Endeavor Convention held in Boston in 1895 far surpassed that of 1892 in numbers if not in enthusiasm, for fifty thousand delegates attended, making it by far the largest in its history up to that time, and probably the largest attempted since then, as it was found that a convention of such proportions must be split up into sections, which was not productive of the best results.

The most eminent speakers and leaders of song available were secured, and everything passed off with great enthusiasm as might be expected where such an aggregation of young people imbued with the spirit of Christian endeavor were gathered.

It was very interesting to note the contrast be-

tween that great gathering and the first convention
of the Society held in Providence in 1878, where
but a few score of people had a part.

The contrast must have been startling to Dr.
Clark, for it is doubtful whether in those early
days his wildest flight of imagination had pictured
what a great world-wide organization his was destined to become. My first meeting with Dr. Clark
was in the year 1877 when he was in his initial
pastorate in Portland, Maine. He was then but a
youth, little dreaming the destiny God was fitting
him for; for, while he must even then have been
a man with a vision, he was never "visionary," but
of rare judgment, as his afterlife has so wonderfully demonstrated.

In those brief years that intervened between
those two conventions, the Society had become an
organization wielding an influence in the churches
with which it was connected that was world-wide,
and already Dr. Clark had been around the world
in its interests, and since then, several times. To
what dimensions the movement has grown in the
more than a score of years since that great convention, I have no present knowledge, but it is fair
to presume that its influence is to-day one of the
greatest agencies of the church at large for the

advancement of the cause of Christianity throughout the world.

The Fiftieth Anniversary of the Founding of
the Young Men's Christian Association in this
country was held in the largest hall in the city.
The responsibility for the conduct of the music
was divided between one of the Y.M.C.A. secre-
taries, Clarence B. Willis, and myself.

This important event in the history of the Association brought together its leading lights from
every part of our country, and not a few from foreign lands.

Perhaps the most prominent visitor from abroad
was Mr. Howard Williams, one of the sons of
George Williams, the honored founder of the
Association, to whom reference has been made.

He came to represent his father, who was then
well advanced in life, and to bring his blessing and
salutations.

With him came Lord Kinnaird, one of the most
celebrated and youthful laymen in Great Britain,
whose presence added much interest to the occasion, as he was known to be a hearty and generous
supporter of the Association in his country.

But the one among the notable array of celebrated men who added most to the interest of the

convention was Booker T. Washington, whose address was the most interesting and entertaining from a popular standpoint.

He was then the most celebrated man of his race, an honored citizen of our country, and a splendid orator. No man of his day could give a more interesting and graphic description of the rise of his people from bondage and ignorance toward civilization, or could better describe their characteristics and dialects. He would often in his inimitable way give illustrations of the latter, not alone to entertain his auditors, but to enforce his statement.

In this connection it will be of interest to relate a bit of history that had a bearing on his future, as showing how great issues are sometimes determined by seemingly trifling events.

Some time in the eighties, an association was formed in New Haven, that came to be known as the "Christian Workers' Convention," which had for its object the awakening of interest in Rescue Missions that were being formed in many of the principal cities of the country. Dr. R. A. Torrey was its president during the several years of its existence, and I was the leader of the singing at its annual convention.

In the making of the program for one of these annual events which was to be held in Atlanta, Georgia, about the year 1889, Booker T. Washington was engaged to deliver a ten-minute address. At the time the convention assembled he was in Boston in the interest of his school at Tuskegee, Alabama, but as he had never addressed an audience of white people in the South, he deemed it of sufficient importance to leave his work and hasten to Atlanta.

When the time for his address came, he was on the platform before an audience of Atlanta citizens that filled the large opera house. As Dr. Torrey introduced him, he arose with some trepidation and for the first time faced a white audience in the Southland, not knowing what his reception might be. He proceeded with his brief address, and when the ten minutes had expired the Governor of the State, who was also on the platform, and who was known for his active interest in religious matters, arose and proposed that Mr. Washington's time be extended. It was put to a vote of the convention and passed unanimously, and his time extended to the gratification and profit of the large audience.

This circumstance served to open the door for the

remainder of Mr. Washington's life to the people of that part of the country, and he was from that time regarded by the best people of his land as among their most distinguished citizens, whose abilities they admired, and whom they looked upon as a benefactor to his race and an honor to his country.

The fifth and last campaign that I was engaged in across the sea was the winter of 1896-7 spent with Major Whittle in Scotland. On this visit we were accompanied by Mrs. Whittle and Mrs. Stebbins, the latter assisting us in the work during that strenuous winter in the land of the Scots.

From a previous visit to that country, accompanied then by Mr. and Mrs. McGranahan, Major Whittle had come to be known and loved by the people and the clergy; so on this second visit he had everywhere a very cordial reception and constant evidences of the affectionate regard in which he was held by the Christians of that country.

The cities visited were Edinburgh, Glasgow, Aberdeen, Inverness and several smaller places.

While in one of the latter we learned of the death of Professor Henry Drummond at Sterling, his home city.

He had been for more than a year a great sufferer from a disease that rendered it impossible for him to move any part of his body save his head and one hand. Yet his attendant, who was a personal friend, and his physician as well, said that during all his long suffering he remained constantly cheerful and uncomplaining, which we could quite believe would be true of a man of his character.

As we had long known him and admired him for his great ability and had loved him for the charm of his personality, we felt constrained to leave our work and join with his host of friends in paying the last tribute of respect and love to him whom God had so richly endowed with gifts that made him a blessing to his fellow men.

This winter abroad proved to be the last extended evangelistic movement that either Major Whittle or I engaged in, as I had some premonitions of a breakdown during the campaign—the result of many years of continued strain. Major Whittle, while then in good health, not long after his return from abroad, gave himself wholeheartedly to the spiritual and physical welfare of the soldiers who were in the Southern camps under training for service in the Spanish war. Forgetting that he was no longer young or able to endure the fatigue and exposure of camp life with the immunity he had once enjoyed, he contracted a disease which undermined his strength to such an extent that he was obliged to retire from public work, for the most part, from that time till his death two or three years afterwards.

Following that winter in Scotland, my public activities were largely confined to convention work and the summer conferences in Northfield; and in the later years, entirely to the latter, which brought me finally in the last years of Mr. Alexander's service there, to the close of two score years of work in my chosen field.

The music of those world-famed conferences from the very beginning in 1889 had been a prominent feature. Mr. Sankey, Mr. McGranahan and myself, were in charge until one after another dropped out. First Mr. McGranahan retired broken in health, then Mr. Sankey; both of whom, after some years of wasting strength, passed away, leaving the responsibility upon me. When Mr. Alexander came in 1915 he shared with me, assuming at once the direction of the more important services, and when the time came for me to pass on to other hands the entire responsibilities, he was

there to undertake them, which gave promise that
the singing for years to come would continue to be
an inspiration to the conferences.

It was not to be under his leadership, however,
as he was called soon afterwards to a higher sphere
of labor. And upon whomsoever shall rest the
mantle laid down by Mr. Alexander, may God
put the seal of His approval.

REMINISCENCES OF CELEBRATED WRITERS AND SINGERS OF GOSPEL SONGS

My acquaintance with some of the early writers of Gospel hymns began in Chicago in 1870, where I had gone in the autumn before to enter the musical profession.

My life up to that time had been spent on a farm in the western part of New York State. Only the name of George F. Root had penetrated that remote region, hence he was the musician of all others I desired most to meet. It was not long before the opportunity came, which marked the beginning of a cordial relation and friendship.

DR. GEORGE F. ROOT

Dr. George F. Root was one of the first musicians of the country to turn his attention to writing the class of Sunday School music originated by William B. Bradbury. And as he was contemporaneous with the latter and associated with him in musical convention and institute work, it may be said that he shared with him the honor of being the first writer of that class of music that has had such an influence upon the life of the church during the last two generations.

He was a voluminous writer of both sacred and secular music, and in the years of his greatest activities edited many publications, which established his reputation as a gifted musician. It was not, however, until the outbreak of the Civil War that he became a national figure, through his contributions to patriotic songs during that crisis in the nation's history. "Just Before the Battle, Mother," "The Battle Cry of Freedom," and others, gave him an enviable place in the esteem of his country, for they were a source of inspiration to soldiers on the field and around the camp fire, as well as to the great cause of freedom throughout the land.

While Dr. Root wrote much for the people, as indicated in the character of his hymns, he was a musician honorably recognized by the profession and was given the degree of Doctor of Music in 1873 by the Chicago University.

He was a man of singularly gracious and engaging personality, and of spiritual convictions, aiming always to inspire others with high ideals both in character and art.

RING THE BELLS OF HEAVEN

REV. W. O. CUSHING   GEO. F. ROOT

Joyfully.

1. Ring the bells of heav-en! there is joy to-day, For a soul re-
2. Ring the bells of heav-en! there is joy to-day, For the wan-d'rer
3. Ring the bells of heav-en! spread the feast to-day, An-gels swell the

D.C.—'Tis th ran-somed ar - my, like a might-y sea, Peal-ing forth the

FINE.

turn-ing from the wild; See! the Fa-ther meets him out up-on the way,
now is re-con-ciled; Yes, a soul is res-cued from his sin-ful way,
glad triumphant strain, Tell the joy-ful tid-ings! bear it far a-way,

an-them of the free.

CHORUS.

Wel-com-ing His wea-ry wand'ring child.
And is born a-new a ransomed child. } Glo-ry! glo-ry! how the
For a pre-cious soul is born a-gain.

D.C.

an - gels sing; Glo - ry! glo - ry! how the loud harps ring,

WRITERS AND SINGERS   187

One incident that impressed this upon my
mind occurred once when I had called upon him at
his home. After some moments of conversation,
he led me to the front of the parlor, where a Bible
lay open on a table, to which he called my attention
with a reverence that left an ineffaceable impression upon me that he regarded the Word of God
as the chart of his life.

I recall with pleasure his kindly attitude toward
me and his words of encouragement at my early
attempts at composition. And later on when I
had done considerable writing I was much heart-
ened by his request that I send him some of my
compositions. Shortly afterward, when the music
of "I've Found a Friend," was written, it was
sent to him in manuscript form in fulfillment of
the promise I had made, and as a slight expression
of appreciation of his kindness to me.

His most popular Sunday School and Gospel
songs were: "When He Cometh," "Come to the
Savior," "Ring the Bells of Heaven," "Why
Not?," "Knocking, Knocking," "Oh, Touch the
Hem of His Garment," "Along the River of
Time," "In the Silent Midnight Watches," and
others.

Dr. Root had a remarkable memory. As an instance: Mr. Charles H. Gabriel told me that one of his first compositions was sent to Dr. Root in 1875 and printed in "The Musical Messenger." In 1893 Mr. Gabriel first met Dr. Root, who immediately said, "Oh, yes! You sent me a manuscript away back in 1875, entitled 'Waiting on the Shore,' and I have wondered about you." So much has been written about this great and good man in addition to his own "Story of my Life," that more cannot be added.

Dr. Root was born August 30, 1820, at Sheffield, Massachusetts, and after an honorable and distinguished career as a man and musician, passed away at Bailey Island, Maine, on August 6, 1895, bringing to a close the life of one who had by his high character and consecration of his superior gifts, brought honor to his profession and to his native land.

Philip Paul Bliss

The first one of the Gospel hymn writers I had the privilege of meeting, with the exception of Dr. Root, was P. P. Bliss. We were living near each other on the west side of Chicago, he on Ann Street and I on Randolph, but a few blocks away. I am unable to recall the time or the occasion of my meeting him, as a half century has since passed, but the impression he made upon me then, and as I came to know him afterwards, does not fade with the passing of time.

He was then engaged in conducting musical conventions throughout the Middle West, and was connected with the music publishing house of Root & Cady. He was also the director of music for the First Congregational Church, on the west side, and subsequently its Sunday School superintendent.

Mr. Bliss began writing for Sunday Schools in the early seventies, and his first book, "The Charm," was published in 1871 by the John Church Co., and the second, "Sunshine," in 1873.

About this time reports were coming from Scotland of the remarkable revival under the direction of Moody and Sankey, which led Mr. Bliss to turn his attention more to writing hymns suitable for evangelistic work than hitherto. It was at this time, also, that he and Major Whittle, through the urgency of Mr. Moody, were led to give up their business and professional pursuits and enter the evangelistic field.

On making this decision, he began the preparation of his book entitled "Gospel Songs," which was his first venture in this field, and in the summer and autumn of 1875 he assisted Mr. Sankey in editing the first book of the series called "Gospel Hymns," and a year following the second number of that series was published.

Several of his celebrated songs and hymns were written for his first book, "Gospel Songs," the most notable of which was "Hold the Fort," which was written upon an incident related by Major Whittle that occurred during the Civil War, when Sherman was on his famous "March to the Sea." The Federal forces were pressing the Confederates hard, and at one point Sherman signaled to one of his commanders: "Hold the fort, for I am coming."

This song sprang at once into great favor both in this country and abroad, as a splendid rally slogan, and has maintained its popularity to the present day.

Some time after this, Mr. Bliss and Major Whittle were engaged in evangelistic work in the South, and at one time they visited Kennesaw Mountain, and on the spot where the famous order was given, he plucked a flower and enclosed it in a letter to Mrs. Stebbins, both of which she carefully preserved as mementoes of him and his thoughtfulness.

My home was then in Boston, where I had gone in 1874, therefore I saw little of him for two or three years, but we kept in touch through correspondence.

In the autumn of that year I was given charge of music in the late Dr. A. J. Gordon's church, and in January, 1876, became director of music in Tremont Temple. In August following I had occasion to spend a few days with Mr. Moody at his home in Northfield and while there became associated with Mr. Sankey and himself in their evangelistic work which lasted until the death of Mr. Moody. I at once resigned my professional work in Boston, and on the 1st of September began the organization of a choir in Chicago to assist in the Moody and Sankey three months' campaign that was to begin the first of October in a tabernacle constructed for the purpose. During the month I was thus engaged I had accommodations at the hotel in which Mr. Bliss was staying and had the opportunity of associating with him.

During his visits there he wrote the music to two of his well known hymns—"It Is Well with My Soul" and "Eternity." In one of his frequent visits to my room he sang for me the latter hymn and I was so much impressed by its solemnity and its striking character that I began to use it in my work at once. It was for years one of our most useful and impressive selections.

It so happened that it was the last song Mr. Bliss ever sang, so far as is known, as it was his closing song in the meetings conducted by Major Whittle in Peoria, from which place he and Mrs. Bliss went directly to Rome, Pennsylvania, to spend the Christmas holidays with their two boys.

It had been arranged by Mr. Moody that Mr. Bliss and Major Whittle should continue the meetings that came to a close at the end of the year in Chicago, holding them on Sundays in the tabernacle and week days in the churches; and it was when he and Mrs. Bliss were on their way from Rome to fill that engagement—on December 29, 1876—that they met their tragic death at Ashtabula.

At that time I was on my way to Portland, Maine, to engage in an evangelistic movement. I was intercepted by a telegram from Mr. Moody recalling me to Chicago to assist Major Whittle in the meetings arranged for Mr. Bliss and himself. I returned immediately, arriving in time to assist in the opening meeting of the series.

At the first meeting after Moody and Sankey had left for Boston, Major Whittle, in referring to the disaster that had caused such an appalling loss of life, mentioned the fact that the last song sung by Mr. Bliss was "Eternity," then announced that it would now be sung at the present meeting.

He had been listened to in breathless silence, and when the hymn beginning with the words, "Oh, the clanging bells of time," and ending with the word, "Eternity," rang out, the feeling had become intense, and a silence brooded over the people that could be felt. So deep was the impression made by the circumstances related, and the singing of the song under conditions prevailing, that it was advertised to be sung every time the services were held in the tabernacle afterwards.

As to Mr. Bliss' place among the writers of Gospel hymns, it has long been admitted that he occupied a preëminence that still stands unrivaled, and to my mind it is a just estimate.

There has been no writer of verse since his time who has shown such a grasp of the fundamental truths of the Gospel, or such a gift for putting them into poetic and singable form as he. Take, for instance, "Hallelujah, What a Savior!" There is in that hymn not only a remarkably clear and forci-

ble presentation of the atonement, but it is put in
words not one of which could be changed for the
better. Nor, indeed, could there have been a more
suitable or sympathetic setting for them than is
found in his admirable music. Another illustration
is to be found in the hymn, "Free from the Law,"
which is conceded to be the clearest statement of the
doctrine of grace in distinction from the law to be
found in hymnology. Indeed, it was said at the
time of Moody and Sankey's first visit to Scotland
in 1873 that the singing of that hymn had more to
do in breaking down the prejudice that existed
against Gospel hymns up to that time than anything else, as its teaching was so Scriptural and in
such perfect accord with the teaching of the Scottish divines. The musical setting of it, too, could
not have been improved upon.

Then, as an illustration of a hymn making a solemn appeal to the undecided, could there be anything more impressive or beautiful than his "Almost
Persuaded," which is, indeed, a classic in its way?

Other compositions could be cited that would illustrate still further his rare gifts, but these are so
representative that it is needless to illustrate
further.

In these hymns, as in all of which he was the

ONCE FOR ALL

P. P. B.

P. P. BLISS

1. Free from the law, O hap-py con-di-tion, Je-sus hath
2. Now are we free—there's no con-dem-na-tion, Je-sus pro-
3. "Chil-dren of God," O glo-ri-ous call-ing, Sure-ly His

bled, and there is re-mis-sion; Cursed by the law and bruised by the
vides a per-fect sal-va-tion; "Come un-to Me," O hear His sweet
grace will keep us from fall-ing; Pass-ing from death to life at His

CHORUS

fall, Grace hath redeemed us once for all.
call, Come, and He saves us once for all.   Once for all, O sin-ner, recall, Bless-ed sal-va-tion once for all.

ceive it, Once for all, O broth-er, be-lieve it; Cling to the

Cross, the bur-den will fall, Christ hath re-deemed us once for all.

author, there was manifest a happy blending of
the poet and musician, and along with it rare judgment and deep spiritual insight into the needs of
presenting the saving truths of Scripture in clear
and singable form.

In my estimation his work in both fields is
worthy to be recognized as an ideal to be followed
by writers of to-day, and I have always held his
sympathetic and appropriate musical settings as a
guide in my own work.

So versatile were Mr. Bliss' talents that his gifts
as singer and leader were little less than those he
possessed as a writer of hymns. He had a voice
of rare quality and splendid volume, a baritone of
extraordinary range and evenness throughout, and
a perfect method of voice production and control,
which enabled him to modulate it at will.

As a leader he occupied a position of prominence
by reason of native gifts and years of experience,
which, combined with an impressive personality (he
was six feet tall and of commanding stature, with
features as perfect in form, and eyes that were
large and kindly in expression), made him the
great leader of evangelistic song that he was.

He sang without ostentation, playing his own
accompaniment on a cabinet organ. His leading

was also without display or any attempt at attracting attention to himself.

P. P. Bliss was born July 9th, 1838, and reared in the country, his birthplace being in Clearfield County, Pennsylvania. His early advantages for the development of his talents were meager, but he made the best use of them possible, and when he had the opportunity to attend musical conventions his strides toward the accomplishment of the ambitions that had been awakened in him became rapid, and he early joined the ranks of the professional convention leaders, becoming one of the most successful and prominent among them.

These achievements, however, were but stepping stones to a greater work God had in store for him, and served to prepare the way to a world-wide ministry of song that was to bless coming generations. What further service he would have accomplished had his life been spared, cannot be known, but the service already rendered is still, after a half century, a blessing and inspiration to untold millions over the world, a monument far more enduring than marble.

THE NINETY AND NINE

ELIZABETH C. CLEPHANE   IRA D. SANKEY

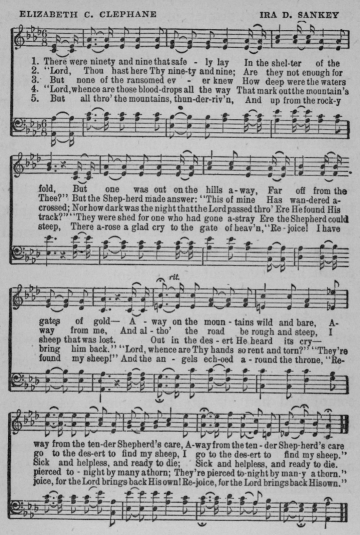

1. There were ninety and nine that safe - ly lay   In the shel-ter   of the
2. "Lord,   Thou hast here Thy nine-ty and nine;   Are they not enough for
3. But   none of the ransomed ev - er knew   How deep were the waters
4. "Lord,whence are those blood-drops all the way   That mark out the mountain's
5. But   all thro' the mountains, thun-der-riv'n,   And up from the rock-y

fold, But   one   was out on the hills a - way, Far off from the
Thee?" But the Shep-herd made answer: "This of mine   Has wan-dered a-
crossed; Nor how dark was the night that the Lord passed thro' Ere He found His
track?" "They were shed for one who had gone a-stray Ere the Shepherd could
steep, There a-rose a glad cry to the gate of heav'n, "Re - joice! I have

rit.

gates of gold— A - way on the moun - tains wild and bare, A-
way from me, And al - tho' the road be rough and steep, I
sheep that was lost.   Out in the des - ert He heard its cry—
bring him back." "Lord, whence are Thy hands so rent and torn?" "They're
found my sheep!" And the an - gels ech-oed a - round the throne, "Re-

way from the ten-der Shepherd's care, A-way from the ten - der Shep-herd's care
go to the des-ert to find my sheep, I go to the des-ert to   find my sheep."
Sick and helpless, and ready to die;   Sick and helpless, and ready to die.
pierced to - night by many a thorn; They're pierced to-night by man-y a thorn."
joice, for the Lord brings back His own! Re-joice, for the Lord brings back His own."

IRA D. SANKEY

Ira D. Sankey was born in the village of Edinburgh, Pennsylvania, August 28th, 1840, where he lived six years. His parents then moved to a place known as Western Reserve Harbor, and soon thereafter located on a farm, where he grew up, assisting in farm work until he was seventeen years of age. In 1857 he, with his parents, removed to New Castle, Pennsylvania, where his father became president of a bank, and where all the family united with the Methodist Church. He took an active interest in the Sunday School of the church, and in due time became the superintendent, and also leader of the church choir.

In 1861, at the call of Abraham Lincoln for volunteers, he enlisted, and while serving in the army was instrumental in interesting the men in forming a musical club, which became known as the "Singing Boys in Blue." When his term of enlistment expired he became assistant to his father, who had been appointed by Mr. Lincoln as a collector of Internal Revenue.

From that time on his services were in demand as a singer at political gatherings and in Sunday School conventions in Western Pennsylvania and Eastern Ohio.

It was while attending the International Y. M. C. A. convention at Indianapolis in 1870 as a delegate, that he first met Mr. Moody, who, after hearing him sing, said to him:

"Where are you from? Are you married? What is your business?" Mr. Sankey told him where he lived, that he was married and had two children and that he was engaged in government employ. Mr. Moody replied, "You will have to give that up and come to Chicago and help me in my work." Mr. Sankey told him he could not give up his business. Mr. Moody said, "You must; I have been looking for you for eight years." He then asked if he would go with him and pray over the matter. Sankey was much impressed by Moody's prayer and promised to take the matter under consideration. After six months of indecision he spent a week with Moody, and before that week was over he sent his resignation to his superior officer and arranged to join Mr. Moody permanently in his work.

He came to Chicago, therefore, in the early part of 1871, to assist D. L. Moody in his important church and mission work on the north side of the city, which had come into existence as the result of many years of untiring and enthusiastic labor.

In addition to his duties as leader of singing in that work, he was engaged with Mr. Moody in evangelistic work elsewhere in the city, and in towns adjacent; also in conducting the Y. M. C. A. daily noon meetings, of which Moody had long been the inspiring and militant leader.

It was at one of those meetings I met Mr. Sankey, and we soon became friends.

Occasionally when attending those meetings I was invited by him to assist in singing some selection, as Mr. Moody, even in those early days before solo singing in special meetings had become an established custom, always had Sankey, or Bliss, when available, sing special selections at every meeting.

During the eighteen months that intervened between Sankey's coming to Chicago and his going abroad with Moody to begin the work that was to make their names household words throughout the Christian world, there was little worthy of note in our relations beyond the ordinary intercourse of friends who occasionally met, save one incident that has ever been memorable to me, and that was his introducing me to Philip Phillips, who was at that time a guest in his home.

While Sankey was engaged with Moody in their

work in Great Britain, I had occasional letters from him couched in the same cordial and friendly terms characteristic of him, with never the slightest intimation that he was conscious of being one of the most talked of men in the Empire; and on his return to his native land after two years of absence in which he had risen from comparative obscurity to world-wide fame, the friendly intercourse was resumed that continued unbroken the remainder of his life.

Prior to the work in which he and Moody were engaged in Great Britain, no other evangelist ever had associated with him a singer who not only assumed the direction of the musical part of the work, but whose name was linked with that of the evangelist as an associate, and everywhere given equal prominence. Nor was there before that movement the title of "Singing Evangelist" ever known. Mr. Sankey was the first to receive that designation, and he, therefore, became the pioneer of the ever growing army of consecrated singers who have for fifty years been following in his train.

Be that as it may, it is quite beyond question that he brought the service of song in evangelistic movements to the front in so striking a manner, demonstrating its importance as an aid in enforcing the

HOME OF THE SOUL

MRS. ELLEN H. GATES

PHILIP PHILLIPS

1. I   will sing you a song of that beau-ti-ful land, The far a-way home
2. O   that home of the soul in my visions and dreams, Its bright, jas-per walls
3. That un-chang-a-ble home is for you and for me, Where Je-sus of Naz-
4. O   how sweet it will be in that beau-ti-ful land So free from all sor-

of the soul, Where no storms ev-er beat on the glit-ter-ing strand, While the years
I can see; Till I fan-cy but thin-ly the veil in-ter-venes Be-tween
ar-eth stands; The King of all kingdoms for-ev-er is He, And He hold-
row and pain, With songs on our lips and with harps in our hands, To meet

of e-ter-ni-ty roll, While the years of e-ter-ni-ty roll; Where no storms
the fair cit-y and me, Be-tween the fair cit-y and me, Till I fan-
eth our crowns in His hands, And He holdeth our crowns in His hands; The King
one an-oth-er a-gain, To meet one an-oth-er a-gain; With songs

ev-er beat on the glit-ter-ing strand, While the years of e-ter-ni-ty roll.
cy but thin-ly the vail in-ter-venes Be-tween the fair cit-y and me.
of all kingdoms for-ev-er is He, And He holdeth our crowns in His hands.
on our lips and with harps in our hands, To meet one an-oth-er a-gain.

claims of the gospel upon the world, that to him belongs the honor of securing for it its rightful place as a divinely appointed agency in proclaiming the Gospel of the Son of God, and establishing the custom of evangelists going about two by two, preacher and singer, preaching the Word in sermon and song.

But in giving Mr. Sankey this honor, it should be said also that Mr. Moody, more than any other evangelist of his time, recognized the powerful influence of inspiring hymns upon the people, and that to him belongs the credit of not only recognizing the fact, but of giving it the place and prominence it has had in all evangelistic movements since that time.

Mr. Moody loved Christian song as few do, even though he was unable to recognize the difference between one tune and another; he always insisted upon having enthusiastic singing, and a great deal of it, as those who were associated with him as leaders could testify from a sense of weariness bordering on exhaustion. He was ever thoughtful of those helping him, however, as it is my pleasure to testify, for he would say to me at the close of a heavy day's work just before beginning his last sermon for the day: "You slip out and go home, for I want you to be fresh for to-morrow." So it must be said that Moody recognized in a very remarkable degree that the singing of the Gospel was one of the greatest agencies in reaching the hearts of the people, and that Sankey demonstrated it in a remarkable way.

Before he entered upon his career as an evangelist he had never attempted to write music suited to evangelistic work, but soon after his work with Mr. Moody assumed such proportions abroad in 1873, he began this phase of his work which from that time forward gave him a place among the foremost writers of Gospel song. His first attempt to write for that purpose was in Edinburgh, Scotland, and the music he then wrote was his setting to Dr. Horatio Bonar's beautiful hymn, "Yet There Is Room." His second attempt was his famous hymn, "I'm Praying for You," which became one of the most useful in all the range of evangelistic hymns, and has been blessed by uncounted multitudes in all parts of the world.

I had loved and often sang the song, but its true worth and simple melody never impressed me as it did on the occasion of one of my visits to him during his last days. I was sitting by his bedside

when he requested his nurse, Mr. Rosewall, to bring
out the phonograph. This, with a liberal variety of
records, had been provided to relieve the monotony
of his days—which were all nights—and among
them was a record of "I'm Praying for You,"
made by an unusually sweet and sympathetic baritone voice. The reproduction was all that could
be desired—every word and tone being distinct
and clear. As I sat there beside the great singer
who had sung his last song till he joined the "Choir
Invisible," the voice seemed to come from the very
gates of heaven—pleading with wanderers on earth
to make Him—"your Savior, too." I was conscious of an experience that comes now and again
in the lives of all who love the songs of heaven and
home, and the beauty of it lingers unchanged by
the passing of years.

Mr. Sankey's subsequent compositions placed
him among the most gifted writers of evangelistic
and devotional music. Among the many of his
hymns that have survived the lapse of time and
are still used in all parts of the world, may be mentioned: "I'm Praying for You," "The Ninety
and Nine," "Hiding in Thee," "Faith Is the Victory," "When the Mists Have Rolled Away,"

"Simply Trusting," "Shelter in the Time of Storm," "Under His Wings" and "There'll Be No Dark Valley."

The one that will be associated with him for possible generations yet to come, is the "Ninety and Nine," for two reasons; first, the words visualize intensely the Shepherd seeking the lost sheep—indeed the climax is almost startling. In the second place, the music (in itself quite inferior to much of Mr. Sankey's writing) is admirably suited to express, in a graphic manner, that rarely beautiful story. Especially did it lend itself to Mr. Sankey's characteristic manner of singing and interpretation.

In describing the origin of the hymn, Sankey relates that when he and Moody were going from Glasgow to Edinburgh, in 1874, he chanced to see the words of the hymn in a newspaper, and it occurred to him it would make a good song for their use, and called Mr. Moody's attention to it. Later in the day they were holding a meeting in the Free Assembly Hall in the latter city. After Moody's address on the Shepherd, he asked Sankey if he had a hymn he could sing on the subject. Recalling nothing, on the spur of the moment, save the hymn found on the train, a voice whispered: "Sing it!"

and, acting upon the suggestion, he took his seat at the organ, placed the words before him, and sang them to the tune that came to him spontaneously. The song became a favorite at once and was used for many years to the awakening and winning back to the fold of uncounted numbers of souls.

Mr. Sankey's knowledge of the art of singing and the use of his voice was intuitive rather than through cultivation, showing that he possessed gifts of an extraordinary character to have accomplished what he did.

His voice was a high baritone of exceptional volume, purity and sympathy. Although he had no special training, he unconsciously acquired the habit of correct tone-production, which enabled him to preserve his voice uninjured through long years of hard usage—even to the end of his public career.

His interpretation of songs was his own conception; and in his rendering of them he always kept before him the importance of making the subject of the hymn stand out in great distinctness, even though it did violence sometimes to the accepted rules of musical phrasing. Seated at a low top organ with which he always accompanied himself he, without ostentation, sang his messages into the hearts and consciences of people in a way that justly made him famous as an interpreter of evangelistic song.

In further accounting for the remarkable influence he exerted through his singing, personality should be taken into consideration. He was forceful, and for want of a better term to describe the indefinable, he was magnetic. He had an attractive face, in which there was sympathy and buoyancy of spirit always manifest. His sincerity in the consecration of his voice to the service of his fellowmen, made him, under God, the great evangel of song that he was.

In addition to the spiritual trend of Mr. Sankey's nature, which was always evidenced in a wholesome and unaffected way, he was one of the most companionable of men and loyal of friends. As was the case with Moody, he had a keen sense of humor,—loved to laugh and to make others laugh by his bright, humorous incidents and stories—a trait that was not lacking even when in later years disease had reduced him to a shadow of his former physique.

I once heard him tell an incident that occurred in his youth. He was one day riding horseback, and as it was raining, he held an umbrella over

O THAT WILL BE GLORY

C. H. G.

CHAS. H. GABRIEL

1. When all my la - bors and tri - als are o'er, And I am safe on that
2. When, by the gift of His in - fi - nite grace, I, am ac - cord - ed in
3. Friends will be there I have loved long a - go; Joy-like a riv - er a -

beau - ti - ful shore, Just to be near the dear Lord I a - dore,
heav - en a place, Just to be there and to look on His face,
round me will flow; Yet, just a smile from my Sav - iour, I know,

Will thro' the a - ges be glo - ry for me, ... O that will be
O . . . . . . that will

CHORUS.

glo - ry for me, Glo - ry for me, glo - ry for me; When by His grace
be glo - ry for me, Glo - ry for me, glo - ry for me; . . . .

I shall look on His face, That will be glo - ry, be glo - ry for me.

him; suddenly his horse took fright, reared and plunged forward entirely from under him, leaving him sitting in the muddy road with the umbrella still over his head. This he told to Mr. Moody, upon whom it made such an impression that he never quite got over laughing, whenever it occurred to him, over his friend's predicament, for he loved nothing better than a joke on Mr. Sankey.

Another amusing experience Mr. Sankey relates in a book he brought out the last year or two of his life, entitled "Sankey's Story of the Gospel Hymns," published by the Sunday School Times Company, in which he gives a brief sketch of his life and work, and from which some of the data herein are taken.

"During all our campaigns abroad, it was our custom to rest on Saturdays, whenever it was convenient. While at Sunderland, one Saturday, we took a cab and drove northward along the sea shore. Coming to an almost perpendicular cliff rising high above the sea, we descended by a stairway to the beach below. For a while we enjoyed ourselves walking along the beach examining the beautiful shells left exposed by the tide which had gone out. Our attention was soon arrested by some one shouting from the top of the cliff. We saw a man wildly beckoning us to return, and on looking around discovered that the tide had filled the channel between us and the stairway. It was clear that we had no time to lose. Mr. Moody suggested that I should plunge in and lead the way to the cliff as soon as possible, which I did, and while doing so, he stood looking on convulsed with laughter at my frantic strides through the water over slippery stones. But I reached a place of safety. Then the tables turned, and it was my opportunity to enjoy a sight not soon forgotten, as my friend slowly and with difficulty waded through the rising tide to the place where I stood. We were to hold a Bible reading that afternoon at 3 o'clock, and, not having time to go to our lodgings for a change of apparel, we proceeded to the place of meeting and held the service in our wet clothing."

Another experience that is of historical interest, specially as it was connected with another famous evangelist, he relates as follows: "When Mr. Moody and I were holding meetings in London in 1874, we took a drive, one Saturday, out to Epping Forest. There we visited a gipsy camp. While stopping to speak to two brothers, who had been converted and were doing good missionary work, a few young gipsy lads came up to our carriage. I put my hand on the head of one boy and said, 'May the Lord make a preacher out of you, my boy.' Fifteen years later, when Gipsy Smith first came to this country, I had the pleasure of taking him about Brooklyn. While passing through Prospect Park, he asked me: 'Do you remember driving out of London one day to Epping Forest?'

"I replied that I did. 'Do you remember a little boy standing by your carriage, and of your putting a hand on his head and saying, "My boy, I hope the Lord will make a preacher out of you"?' 'Yes,' I replied, 'I remember it very well.' 'I am that boy,' said Gipsy. My surprise can better be imagined than described, for little did I think that the successful evangelist and fine singer of whom I had heard so much, and whom I admired, was that little boy I had met at the gipsy camp."

Another very striking incident occurred that illustrates in a very graphic way the extraordinary favor he and Mr. Moody enjoyed in Great Britain during that memorable campaign of 1873-1875: An actor at the Royal Theatre in Manchester, England, one night sang a doggerel beginning with the words, "We know that Moody and Sankey are doing some good in their way." It received cheers

and hisses from the audience at first, but on a repetition of the words the manifestation of displeasure
was so great that the comedian was obliged to leave
the stage. Also at a circus in Dublin, on one occasion, one clown said to another: "I feel Moody
to-night," and the other said, "I feel Sankeymoni-
ous." This byplay was not only met with hisses,
but the whole audience arose and joined with tremendous effect in singing one of our hymns, "Hold
the Fort, for I Am Coming."

The last work of importance undertaken by Mr.
Sankey was in the winter of 1898-99 in Great
Britain, where he conducted services of "Sacred
Song and Story" in thirty cities and towns,
which were everywhere attended by throngs.
On his return to this country he became conscious
that he had overtaxed his strength, and from that
time on during the years that remained, he attempted no work of an exacting nature, giving only
an occasional service of song and assisting in the
music at Northfield.

His work abroad undermined his strong constitution, and a gradual decline set in that could not
be arrested. About two years before his death his
sight failed, and total blindness followed in a comparatively short time.

My relations with Mr. Sankey began in 1876, when I became associated with the evangelists, and grew into the closest friendship when we, with James McGranahan, became editors of the series of "Gospel Hymns" as used in the Moody campaigns. In the early eighties we became closely adjoining residents of Brooklyn, which brought us frequently together as neighbors and friends.

Those years of fellowship in the work were memorable ones—being the years of greatest activities in this country of the evangelists and those associated in their work.

During the last two years of Mr. Sankey's life I visited him every few days, and we had delightful times reviewing experiences of the past. In spite of his emaciated condition and his total blindness, he was ever the same cordial and companionable friend he had always been. His humor would often manifest itself in recalling some amusing incident, laughing as he told it, apparently enjoying to the full each scene as he lived it over again.

But it was plain to be seen that his mind and heart had long been set on his home-going, for the subject would so often intrude our conversations. Once he said, "George, you will find me on Spurgeon Street, when you get up there." And often at the close of a visit did he say: "George, I want you to be at the church next Sunday, (the church known as Dr. Cuyler's, of which he had been a member for many years) for I'll be there, as I am going home."

He had so longed to be "absent from the body and present with the Lord," that his passing had become an obsession with him.

That time came in August of 1908. I was at Northfield conducting the singing at the annual conference—a work he and I had done yearly from the beginning of those occasions in 1880—but I was "at the church" when he was taken there to receive the last marks of affection and love from his host of friends and looked for the last time upon the face of the great singer who had gone to join the choir of the redeemed on high.

PHILIP PHILLIPS

I had heard much of Mr. Phillips for years, even before leaving the old home; especially of his singing his famous song, "Home of the Soul," and the privilege of meeting him, therefore, was one of the jewels of those early years.

At that time Mr. Sankey had under consideration a proposition to accompany Mr. Phillips to the Pacific Coast to assist him in sacred concerts, for which he was offered flattering pecuniary rewards.

He had also under consideration Mr. Moody's plan for him to go to England, which was an attractive proposition, both of which were quite naturally within the scope of his ambition, and so appealing that it was hard for him to decide. But the world soon learned how they were settled, for he was divinely led in the choice he made.

Philip Phillips went on his way demonstrating his right to the title he long had borne as the "Singing Pilgrim," and Mr. Sankey fared forth singing the Gospel to unnumbered multitudes on the other side of the sea in his inimitable manner, waking a continent to the power of Gospel song it had never before realized.

James McGranahan

Dramatic in its setting was the first meeting of Major Whittle and Mr. McGranahan, men who were destined to become known and loved on two continents.

They had each gone to Ashtabula in what proved

to be a vain quest for some trace of their mutual friends, Mr. and Mrs. P. P. Bliss, who had lost their lives in one of the greatest railway disasters in our country's history. Mr. McGranahan, recognizing the Major, although they were strangers to each other, stepped up to him and said: "Mr. Bliss was one of my dearest friends; my name is McGranahan."

Mr. Bliss had frequently spoken to the Major of McGranahan as being a man who should devote his talent to the Lord's work. These facts flashed to mind as the salutation was given, and he said to himself, "Here stands the very man that is needed to take Mr. Bliss' place." He invited McGranahan to visit him in Chicago where he was conducting the meetings inaugurated by Moody and Sankey—they having gone on to their next campaign. McGranahan accepted the invitation, and I well remember his coming and the pleasure it gave me to meet him. I was there assisting the Major in the meetings referred to.

During Mr. McGranahan's visit he realized that he had come to the parting of the ways in his career, and that it was necessary for him to make choice between continuing the pursuit of his profession or entering the evangelistic field. That it

was a difficult problem to solve may be judged by
the fact that he had up to that time made a flattering success in his convention and institute work;
and to leave it for an untried field in which he
greatly doubted his fitness, made it doubly difficult
for him to choose. He made it a matter of prayer,
however, and was providentially led to resign his
professional duties and devote the rest of his life to
the spread of the Gospel by voice and pen.

At the close of the meetings we were then engaged in, he joined Major Whittle, taking the place
Mr. Bliss had so acceptably filled, and continued
with him for ten years in this country and Great
Britain, when his failing health obliged him to retire from all public activities.

Mr. McGranahan's entering at that time upon
this phase of his career was timely, as there were
few efficient leaders and singers to supply the in-
creasing demand for men qualified to assist evangelists. He also came to it well equipped as a leader
and trainer of choirs, and as a soloist and writer—
in all of which he proved to be an outstanding figure in the ranks of evangelists, and a great acquisition to their forces.

While on the visit to Chicago referred to, he
wrote the music of "My Redeemer," the words of

which were found with other manuscripts in Mr.
Bliss' trunk that escaped the wreck at Ashtabula.
Before his leaving Chicago it was decided to have
it sung in the tabernacle services, and also that it
would be well to have it sung by four men's voices.
The music was arranged accordingly and two of the
most prominent baritone soloists of the city were
secured, they singing the lower parts, Mr. Mc-
Granahan taking the alto, an octave higher, and I
the melody.

A great audience was present in the tabernacle.
The Major related the finding of the words among
Mr. Bliss' effects, and Mr. McGranahan's setting
them to music, which awakened a keen interest
among the people, thus preparing the way for a
sympathetic hearing. The music was attractive
and lent itself readily to an arrangement for male
voices, which happily in this instance blended admirably, and the words were all the more impressive
as being—practically—Mr. Bliss' dying testimony
to what Christ was to him.

The singing of the new song under those circumstances served to launch it on its world-wide mission of praise to the Redeemer.

I recall very vividly an experience I had with
this hymn some months after the music was com-

posed. I had been singing it a great deal in New England, and near the close of our meetings in one city, an Edison phonograph—the most startling invention of that age—was being exhibited. It was suggested that if I could be secured to sing into it and the fact made known in the community, it might serve to bring a larger number of people to the entertainment. I was accordingly invited to "make a record," as it is now called, which I did in the hall where the meetings had recently been held, and the selection I chose was "My Redeemer."

The record was made on a cylinder wrapped in tinfoil, which was turned by hand both in recording and reproducing, as the mechanical device now in use had not been provided at that time, and when it was made I stepped aside and heard myself sing.

I remember as if it were but yesterday the novel experience, as I had never seen a phonograph before, and the hearing of my own voice, and every word with striking distinctness enunciated, and even my characteristic manner of singing, modulation of voice and phrasing, produced a unique sensation.

As Mr. Moody was the recognized leader of the evangelistic movement that had its beginning in

Great Britain in the early seventies, and which continued on this side the sea for some years afterwards, he had associated with him a number of evangelists whose movements were more or less subject to his control. This came to be the case with Mr. McGranahan, as it was mine from the beginning of my connection with the movement in 1876, a year prior to his joining.

He began writing at once, and it soon became evident that he would be a valuable accession to the editorial staff when other books were to be compiled.

Mr. McGranahan's hymns came into popular favor at once, which made a very important addition to the comparatively limited number of new hymns available that were suited to evangelistic work. He was not a prolific writer, as that phrase is understood. The most notable features of his work, as a composer, were originality as expressed in his attractive and flowing melodies, his musicianly skill in the treatment of his themes, and painstaking care in adapting his music to the truth to be sung.

His hymns were in great favor at home and abroad, and are still used, although nearly two generations have passed, which speaks well for their enduring qualities. As an illustration from my own experience of their popularity on the other side of the sea may be cited an incident that occurred when I was assisting Mr. Moody in the fall of 1892, his last work abroad. We had been holding meetings in the principal cities in England, closing with a ten days' mission in Spurgeon's Tabernacle in London. During one of those meetings Mr. Moody received from the present Queen (then Princess May of Teck, who, with her mother, the Duchess of Teck, were in the audience) a request that I sing Mr. McGranahan's beautiful hymn, "Sometime We'll Understand." The request was complied with.

This incident is interesting for two reasons, first, as illustrating the favor with which our hymns were received in that country; and, second, as an indication that they have found their way into the palaces of Royalty, as into the homes of the people. It may be mentioned also as indicating the interest the present Queen of that great Empire takes in religious matters.

Of the number of Mr. McGranahan's hymns that have been held in popular favor for so many years, and still are, may be cited:

"My Redeemer," "Sometime We'll Understand," "Shall You, Shall I?" "There Shall Be Showers of Blessing," "Are You Coming Home To-night?" "I Shall Be Satisfied," "Behold, What Manner of Love," "Hallelujah for the Cross," "The Crowning Day Is Coming," and "That Will Be Heaven for Me."

In Mr. McGranahan's personality there were combined many graces that go to make up a well-rounded character; among which were a gentleness and cheerfulness and an unaffected simplicity of nature that made him by the grace of God the lovable and attractive man he was, and that won for him the friendship of all who knew him. In his career as an evangelist he impressed those who came under his influence as being a man not only endowed with rare gifts, but one singularly pure in character, with a simple, unwavering faith in his Lord and in the work committed to him.

James McGranahan was born July 4, 1840, in Pennsylvania, near Adamsville, and spent his boy-hood on a farm. During those years he obtained his first instruction in music in a country "singing school," such as was in vogue in those years. In the same manner, Sankey, Bliss, myself and many others learned to "read notes," for it was my good fortune to have had the unique pleasure of attend-

ing those never-to-be-forgotten evenings of song,
which attracted the young people for miles around.
From this beginning I became a teacher, as did Mc-
Granahan, who became noted as the most prominent singing master in that part of the state. From
this line of work he later entered the field as a
leader of conventions, and in the course of time became associated with Dr. George F. Root and
other eminent teachers in their summer Institute
work.

During his preparation for this latter work, he
studied voice under Bassini, and harmony with
J. C. D. Parker, and later with George Macfarren
of London. His voice was a tenor of rare sweetness and purity, and was considered one of great
dramatic possibilities. He, therefore, brought to
the field of evangelism a beautiful and well-trained
voice, a superior ability as a conductor of singing,
and a rare talent as a composer, and laid them at
the feet of his Lord.

As already stated, after ten years of active labor in the evangelistic field, he was forced by failing health to retire to private life. His remaining
years, even to the last, were spent in writing songs
for his Master's use.

He passed away July 9, 1907, at his home at

Kinsman, Ohio, at the age of sixty-seven years, serene in his confidence in the grace of God and in His written words, resting upon his favorite verse, "Verily, verily, I say unto you, he that believeth on me hath everlasting life." John 6: 47.

REVEREND ROBERT LOWRY, D.D.

Among those noted as composers of Sunday school, evangelistic and devotional music, no name is better known than that of Robert Lowry.

Upon the death of William B. Bradbury in 1868, Dr. Lowry succeeded as editor of Sunday School song books published by Bigelow & Main. After his first book, entitled "Bright Jewels," appeared, William H. Doane became associated with him on a series of books, among which were "Pure Gold," "Royal Diadems," "Welcome Tidings," "Brightest and Best," "Glad Refrain," "Good as Gold," "Joyful Lays," "Fountain of Song," "Bright Array," and others which attained wide circulation among the churches. And from that time on, for many years, the names of Lowry and Doane were household words in the Sunday Schools of the land.

In early life Dr. Lowry prepared for and en-

SHALL WE GATHER AT THE RIVER?

R. L.

ROBERT LOWRY

1. Shall we gath-er at the riv - er, Where bright angel feet have trod;
2. 'On the mar-gin of the riv - er, Wash-ing up its sil - ver spray;
3. Ere we reach the shining riv - er, Lay we ev - 'ry bur-den down.
4. Soon we'll reach the shining riv - er, Soon our pil-grim-age will cease;

With its cry-stal tide for - ev - er Flowing from the throne of God.
We shall walk and worship ev - er, All the hap - py gold - en day.
Grace our spir- its will de - liv - er And pro-vide a robe and crown.
Soon our hap- py hearts will quiv-er With the mel - o-day of peace.

CHORUS.

Yes, we'll gath-er at the riv - er, The beautiful, the beautiful riv - er;

Gather with the saints at the riv - er That flows from the throne of God.

tered the ministry of the Baptist denomination, and in the course of his ministerial labors occupied prominent pastorates in New York City, Brooklyn, Plainfield, and other cities, where he was known for his scholarly attainments. For some years during one of his pastorates he occupied the Chair of Letters in the university of which he was a graduate, and from which institution he received—in 1875—the degree of D.D.

Among the gifts with which he was endowed was a love for music and a talent for composition. Being in touch with the religious movements of the times, and an observer of the trend of events, he early caught Mr. Bradbury's vision of the possibilities of the new Sunday School music, began writing, and soon entered actively upon his career as one of its most successful composers. From this time forward his activities were divided between pastoral duties, composition and editing.

He was author of both words and music of many of his best known songs. "Shall We Gather at the River?" is justly one of the most beautiful, as it is one of the most famous Sunday School songs ever written. "Where Is My Wandering Boy To-night?" is one of the most useful and celebrated of evangelistic songs, giving expression to the cry of broken-hearted fathers and mothers the world over. Others having rank among his best loved are: "I Need Thee Every Hour," "One More Day's Work for Jesus," "Savior, Thy Dying Love," "The Mistakes of My Life Have Been Many," "Marching to Zion," "Nothing but the Blood," and "Up from the Grave He Arose."

A touching incident, illustrating how well known and loved is the beautiful hymn, "Shall We Gather at the River?" is related by an American woman writing from Cairo, Egypt, who was allowed to visit the Military Hospital there soon after some wounded men had been brought in. She says:

"The three hours we could stay were full of work for heart and hand. One young soldier from a Highland regiment excited my interest. He had lost a limb, and the doctor said he would not live through the night. I stopped at his side to see if there was anything I could do for him. He lay with his eyes closed, and as his lips moved I caught the words, 'Mother, mother.' I dipped my handkerchief in a basin of ice water and bathed his forehead where the fever flush burned. 'Oh, that is good!' he said, opening his eyes. Seeing me bending over him, he caught my hand and kissed it. 'Thank you, lady,' he said, 'it 'minds me o' mother.' I asked

him if I could write to his mother. 'No,' he said,
'the surgeon has promised to write, but can you,
will you sing to me?' I hesitated a moment and
looked around. The gleam on the water of the
Nile, as the western rays slanted down, caught my
eye and suggested the 'river the streams whereof
shall make glad the city of God.' I began softly
to sing the Gospel hymn, 'Shall We Gather
at the River?' Eager heads were raised around
us to listen more intently, while bass and tenor
voices, weak and tremulous, came in on the chorus—

> " 'Yes, we'll gather at the river,
>   The beautiful, the beautiful river;
>   Gather with the saints at the river
>   That flows by the throne of God.'

"When the song was ended, I looked into the
face of the boy—for he was not over twenty—and
asked, 'Shall you be there?' 'Yes, I'll be there,
through what the Lord Jesus has done for me,' he
answered, while a 'light that never was on sea or
land' radiated his face. The tears gathered in my
eyes as I thought of the mother in her far-off
Scottish home, watching and waiting for her soldier boy, who was breathing away his life in an
Egyptian hospital. 'Come again, lady, come

again,' I heard on all sides as I left the barracks. I shall go, but I shall not find my Scottish laddie, for by to-morrow's reveille he will have crossed the river."

The following incident regarding "Where Is My Wandering Boy To-night?" is typical of many others that could be related showing how the song has been used, perhaps more than any other, to win back wandering boys.

Chancellor Sims relates that he was once traveling with a man from the West who was on his way to visit his father, whom he had left years before when a boy. There had been trouble between them, and the father had told the son that he could go. In his anger the boy said that he would, and that he would never return. He had gone West and become a wealthy land owner; but he had never written his father and had held anger in his heart all those years. He told how it came about that he was then returning. "A train on which I was traveling became snowed in, and people living nearby made up a load of provisions for the imprisoned passengers. It was discovered that Mr. Sankey was on board, and at the request of the passengers he came out on the platform and sang 'Where Is My Wandering Boy To-night?' That song touched my heart, led me to God, and I am now on my way East to seek reconciliation with my parents."

I had the pleasure of knowing Dr. Lowry but slightly, having met him a few times only; but I loved and sang his songs for many years, and count it an honor to be included in the host of his friends who have long recognized his position as a composer and author of great ability, and who has left a priceless legacy to the cause to which he consecrated his rare gifts.

Dr. Lowry was born in Philadelphia, March 12, 1826, and after a life of distinction as a scholar and minister of the churches he served and of conspicuous service rendered to the ministry of sacred song, he passed away at his home in Plainfield, New Jersey, November 25, 1899, in the 74th year of his age.

Dr. William Howard Doane

Dr. William Howard Doane was born at Preston, Connecticut, February 3, 1834. Early in life he manifested an unusual talent for music and a decided gift for composition.

At the early age of 18, he was elected conductor

of the Norwich Harmonic Society, and ten years later issued his first hymn book, "Sabbath School Gems." This was followed in 1864 by "Little Gems," in 1867 by "Silver Spray," and in 1868 by "Songs of Devotion." He then became associated with Dr. Robert Lowry in editing a series of Sunday School song books.

Dr. Doane was noted also for a series of Christmas cantatas he brought out during those years, which, like his song books, attained great popular favor.

Among his best known songs, a large number were admirably adapted to evangelistic and devotional purposes, such as: "Safe in the Arms of Jesus," "Tell Me the Old, Old Story," "More Love to Thee, O Christ," "Pass Me Not, O Gentle Savior," "I Am Thine, O Lord," "Savior, More Than Life to Me," "Jesus, Keep Me Near the Cross," "Rescue the Perishing," and many others.

Concerning the origin of the most famous and perhaps the best loved of his compositions—"Safe in the Arms of Jesus"—the following story has been told:

"Dr. Doane one day came into the office of Bigelow & Main in New York, and, finding Fanny Crosby there in conversation with Mr. Bradbury,

SAFE IN THE ARMS OF JESUS

FANNY J. CROSBY

W. H. DOANE

1. Safe in the arms of Je - sus, Safe on His gen - tle breast—
2. Safe in the arms of Je - sus, Safe from cor-rod - ing care;
3. Je - sus, my heart's dear ref - uge, Je - sus has died for me;

FINE.

There by His love o'er - shad - ed, Sweet-ly my soul shall rest.
Safe from the world's temp-ta - tions, Sin can-not harm me there.
Firm on the Rock of A - ges, Ev - er my trust shall be.

Hark! 'tis the voice of an - gels, Borne in a song to me,
Free from the blight of sor - row, Free from my doubts and fears;
Here let me wait with pa - tience, Wait till the night is o'er;

D. C. Chorus first four lines.

O - ver the fields of glo - ry, O - ver the jas - per sea.
On - ly a few more tri - als, On - ly a few more tears.
Wait till I see the morn - ing, Break on the gold - en shore.

Used by permission.

WILLIAM H. DOANE AND HUBERT P. MAIN

D. B. TOWNER

he said to her: 'Fanny, I have just written a tune, and I want you to write a hymn for it.' 'Let me hear it,' she requested. Seating himself at a small organ, Mr. Doane played the music through, when she exclaimed: 'Why, that tune says, "Safe in the arms of Jesus," and I will see what I can do about it.' She retired to an adjoining room and in an half hour returned and repeated to him the words of that immortal hymn. It was first published in 'Songs of Devotion,' in 1868, and immediately became popular, was soon published abroad, and is said to be one of the first hymns of its kind to be translated into a foreign language."

In his "Story of Hymns," Mr. Sankey relates a number of very touching incidents in connection with its use.

Of Dr. Doane's other justly famous song— "Rescue the Perishing"—(the words of which also were written by Fanny Crosby) a striking story is told of a drunken man of middle age who staggered into the Bowery Mission one stormy evening, unwashed, unshaved, and wretchedly attired. Sinking into a seat he gazed about, wondering what kind of a place he had gotten into. "Rescue the Perishing" and other Gospel hymns were sung, and he became interested; his brain began to function rationally; memory carried him back to his youth—long forgotten—and tears came to his eyes as he listened to the words of the speaker who was telling the simple story of the Gospel, and how the Lord came to seek and save sinners. In the course of his remarks the leader mentioned several incidents which had occurred in his experience during the Civil War, and mentioned the name of the company in which he had served. At the close of the meeting the man eagerly staggered up to the leader and in a broken voice said: "When were you in that company you spoke of?" "Why, all through the war," was the answer. "Do you remember the battle of ——?" "Perfectly." "Do you remember the name of the captain of your company?" "Yes, his name was ——." "You are right; I am that man! I was your captain. Look at me to-day and see what a wreck I am. Can you save your captain? I have lost everything through drink, and I don't know where to go."

He was saved that night and was helped to get back his old position, became a zealous worker in Rescue Missions, and often told the story of how a soldier saved his captain, and how he loved the words of "Rescue the Perishing."

In 1850 Dr. Doane entered the firm of J. A.

Fay & Co., manufacturers of machinery, whose headquarters were in Norwich, Conn., and in 1860 became the managing partner, with offices at Cincinnati, Ohio, where he made his home the remainder of his active business life.

Devoted as he was to music and its composition, which amounted to almost a life work, it interfered in no way with his success in business, or of his giving great thought and time to church, missionary, Y.M.C.A., Y.W.C.A., and other philanthropic enterprises.

My relations with this good man were cordial and extended over a period of many years. While engaged in an evangelistic campaign in Cincinnati, I had the pleasure of dining with him and his interesting family in their hospitable home.

In 1875 Dr. Doane was given the degree of Doctor of Music by the Dennison University, an honor well deserved, for he served the cause of sacred song with conspicuous ability, placing the church of Christ under lasting obligations to him. He was held in high esteem in his home city because of his philanthropy and public spirit, and for his service to the cause of Christianity.

Dr. Doane, whose service to the cause of worldwide evangelism was so evidently wrought in God, and whose songs will go on blessing generations yet to come, died at his home in Orange, New Jersey, December 23, 1915, at the age of eighty-one.

DR. H. R. PALMER.

On my arrival in Chicago in the autumn of 1869, I occupied a suite of rooms over a grocery store, on the corner of Randolph and May Streets.

Not far away were two large and important churches of the city—the First Congregational and the Second Baptist. Of the former, Dr. Goodwin, the most noted minister of his denomination in the West, was pastor, and Mr. Bliss was the choirmaster and leader of the singing in the Sunday School, of which he at one time was Superintendent. Of the latter, Dr. Goodspeed, a man prominent in his denomination, was pastor, and Dr. Palmer its choirmaster. As I was without permanent church engagement, I worshiped in various churches, hearing their ministers and listening to the music of their choirs.

Dr. Palmer's choir was a very large one, made up from the church membership, and their splendid singing surpassed anything I had heard up to that time.

GALILEE

ROBERT MORRIS, LL.D.   H. R. PALMER

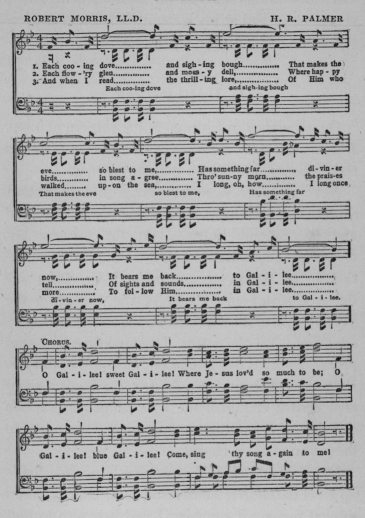

1. Each coo - ing dove............... and sigh - ing bough............... That makes the
2. Each flow - 'ry glen............... and moss - y dell,............... Where hap - py
3. And when I read............... the thrill - ing lore,............... Of Him who
Each coo-ing dove   and sigh-ing bough

eve............... so blest to me,............... Has something far............... di - vin - er
birds............... in song a - gree............... Thro' sun-ny morn,............... the prais-es
walked............... up - on the sea,............... I long, oh, how............... I long once
That makes the eve   so blest to me,   Has something far

now,............... It bears me back............... to Gal - i - lee.
tell............... Of sights and sounds............... in Gal - i - lee...............
more............... To fol - low Him............... in Gal - i - lee...............
di - vin - er now,   It bears me back   to Gal - i - lee.

CHORUS.

O Gal - i - lee! sweet Gal - i - lee! Where Je - sus lov'd so much to be; O

Gal - i - lee! blue Gal - i - lee! Come, sing thy song a - gain to me!

I knew little of Dr. Palmer and less of the nature of his public work, but he soon became recognized throughout the country as one of the foremost conductors of conventions and festivals, and also as a writer of choruses, anthems and songs. One selection his choir in Chicago sang I loved and remembered, was his own popular song, "Galilee."

He was at that time editor of a monthly musical journal called, "The Concordia," published in Chicago. It was also in the early seventies that he published his two books entitled, "The Song Queen," and "The Song King."

Dr. Palmer wrote extensively along technical lines, as is indicated by his bringing out later his "Theory of Music," "Manual for Teachers," "Dictionary of Musical Terms," etc. His writing covered a wide range—singing school, day school, Sunday School, evangelistic, choir and chorus pieces for use in musical convention and festival. He edited some fifty publications, besides writing many secular songs that appeared in sheet form, all of which had a large sale.

He will be remembered, however, by such songs as "Yield Not to Temptation," "Peace, Be Still," and "Come, Sinner, Come."

Among the public activities that brought Dr.

Palmer into great prominence was his direction of the music at the original Chautauqua, founded by the late Bishop John H. Vincent, in the year 1874, at Chautauqua Lake, New York. He conducted with great acceptance and efficiency for fourteen years, making the musical feature one of the special attractions of that famous place.

His work as conductor of conventions, festivals and institutes in many states of the Union and Canada, absorbed much of his energies for the larger part of his career, he laying down the baton only a few weeks before death claimed him.

No incident worthy of record marked my acquaintance with Dr. Palmer in Chicago in 1870. He removed to New York City in 1873, where, after I located in Brooklyn, I occasionally met him at the office of Bigelow & Main, or at some public function. Our last meeting was in Jerusalem, where we were guests of the American Colony. He preceded me to Nazareth and Tiberias, and his visit to the scene of our Lord's life became the inspiration for his famous song, "Galilee, Blue Galilee," of which he wrote both words and music.

Dr. Palmer's most notable work in connection with church choirs began after he became a resident in New York, where he organized the "Church

Choral Union," which had for its object the raising of the standard of music in the churches. The work began in a small way, but like all successful movements, in time it assumed large proportions and appealed to the Protestant churches generally throughout the city. At the height of its success it enrolled twenty thousand singers, nearly four thousand of whom formed the choir at one of the concerts in Madison Square Garden, under Dr. Palmer's direction. The remaining space of the great auditorium (which is said to accommodate nearly twenty thousand people) was crowded with representatives of the more than two hundred churches affiliated with the movement.

In recognition of his services as a musician and an educator of the people to a better appreciation of the art of music, he was honored by Chicago University and Alfred University with the degree of Doctor of Music.

Dr. Palmer was endowed not only with an extraordinary love and talent for music, but with an enthusiastic nature that surmounted all obstacles in the way of his accomplishing any objects he had in view. His was a magnetic personality that enabled him to impart his enthusiasm to choruses. What a pleasure it always was to meet him! How his keen eyes and earnest, smiling expression held you as with a grip and left you with a feeling akin to his own enthusiasm.

Dr. Palmer was born in Sherburne, New York, April 26, 1834, and it is related of him that he sang in his father's choir at nine years of age, and later became organist and choirmaster of the Baptist church in Rushford and Principal of Music of Rushford Academy.

His writings, from the standpoint of quantity and quality, were unsurpassed among musicians during those years, and his text-books are in constant demand to-day.

Dr. Horatius R. Palmer, educator, musician, indefatigable in labor, honored by universities, admired as a Christian gentleman by a host of friends, and loved by all who knew him, passed away at his home at Park-Hill-on-Hudson, November 15, 1907, in his seventy-third year.

Dr. Daniel B. Towner

My first meeting with Dr. Towner was in the summer of 1886, when he came to Northfield to attend the general conference there. Mr. Moody had met him some time previously in Kentucky,

and was so much pleased with his leadership
and singing that, following an invitation to Northfield, he became a member of that group of singers
and evangelists associated in the Master's cause.

The College Student Conference met that year,
its sessions being held at Mount Hermon, the seat
of the Boys' School, and Dr. Towner was selected
to lead the singing. As that first conference
proved of so much interest, it was followed the next
year by another, and as each was of so much profit
to the students, it was decided by the International
Committee of the Young Men's Christian Association having it in charge to make it an annual meeting. The accommodations at Hermon were not
adequate to the growing number of students attending, and the meetings were transferred to
Northfield where for many years thereafter they
were held.

It may be of interest to state that among the first
delegates to these conferences were Robert E.
Speer and John R. Mott, both of whom because
of their extraordinary ability became distinguished
throughout the Christian world.

Mr. Moody presided at those meetings, to which
there was always a deeply serious and spiritual
tone; at the same time never forgetting that he was

once a young man, and that there should be some part of the day for recreation and games, so necessary to the delegation. On those occasions Mr. Moody was heart and soul with them, which had the effect of establishing him in their confidence and admiration. He was a great factor in impressing God's claims upon those young men, and his influence in their subsequent lives can never be measured.

It may here be noted that the General Conference for the deepening of the spiritual life had its beginning in the summer of 1882, at Northfield, and was the first of its kind ever held in this country. It was followed by many others, held in different States. It is of interest, too, that soon after the Student Conference became so helpful to young men, the International Committee of the Young Women's Christian Association decided to have a conference for young women college students, and as in the former case, it was the beginning of a movement along similar lines that spread all over the land. Mr. Moody presided at the sessions of this conference also and was an inspiration to the young women from year to year.

Another movement that had its beginning at Mount Hermon simultaneously with the Student

TRUST AND OBEY

REV. J. H. SAMMIS   D. B. TOWNER

1 When we walk with the Lord   In the light of His word,   What a glo-ry He
2 Not   a shad-ow can rise,'   Not a cloud in the skies,   But His smile quickly
3 Not   a bur-den we bear,·   Not a sor-row we share,   But our toil He doth
4 But   we nev-er can prove   The de-lights of His love,   Un-til all on the
5 Then in fel-low-ship sweet   We will sit at His feet,   Or we'll walk by His

sheds on our way!   While we do His good will,   He a-bides with us still,
drives it a-way;   Not a doubt nor a fear,   Not a sigh nor a tear,
rich-ly re-pay;   Not a grief nor a loss,   Not a frown nor a cross,
al-tar we lay,   For the fa-vor He shows,   And the joy He be-stows,
side in the way;   What He says we will do,   Where He sends we will go,

CHORUS.

And with all who will trust and o-bey.
Can a-bide while we trust and o-bey.
But is blest if we trust and o-bey.   Trust and o-bey, for there's
Are for them who will trust and o-bey.
Nev-er fear, on-ly trust and o-bey.

no oth-er way   To be hap-py in Je-sus, but to trust and o-bey.

Copyright, 1887, by D. B. Towner. Used by permission.

Conference, is the "Student Volunteer Movement," since become one of the greatest factors in the history of Foreign Missions. To perpetuate this event there has been erected in the school room at Hermon, where it had its beginning, a bronze tablet with the following inscription:

"In this room in the month of July, 1886, during the First International Student Conference, the Student Volunteer Movement had Its Origin, and One Hundred Young Men Signified their Willingness and Desire, God Permitting, to Become Foreign Missionaries."

Dr. Towner continued for some years to conduct the singing for the Young Men's Conferences, and later, when the order was established, it became a part of my summer's work to conduct the singing for the Young Women's Conference. For some years Dr. Towner made Northfield his home, and always very acceptably to the people. It was during those summers at Northfield that I saw most of him, and where our friendship began.

An amusing experience in which Dr. Towner had a part illustrates Mr. Moody's habit of making use of his friends whenever they were available. He had an appointment to preach, one Sunday morning, in a little church a few miles from Northfield and insisted that Mr. Sankey, Dr. Towner and myself accompany him and sing. Arriving at the church we entered in single file, Mr. Moody leading, Sankey, Towner and myself following. There was a perfect gradation of stature—Mr. Moody being the shortest, probably about five feet eight, Mr. Sankey two inches taller, and I two inches taller than he, with Dr. Towner still two above me—a coincidence that caused a smile to spread over many faces.

Dr. Towner, like the other singers who were more or less under Mr. Moody's direction, occasionally assisted him in meetings when Mr. Sankey was not available; at other times he assisted in meetings conducted by others of the associated evangelists.

In 1893 Dr. Towner became director of the musical department of what has since become known as the "Moody Bible Institute" in Chicago, a position of responsibility he held until his death. Through his teaching and personal contact he impressed himself upon thousands of young men and women, who have gone out from that institution more or less imbued with the spirit of consecration he ever manifested, and with increased knowledge of the importance of music in all kinds of Christian activities.

During those years Dr. Towner wrote extensively, principally for the books he edited, and from the large number of songs that bear his name there are many that have become known the world over. "Trust and Obey," "Anywhere with Jesus," "Saving Grace," "Full Surrender," "Redeemed," and "Grace Is Greater Than Our Sin," are among his best and most useful compositions.

The origin of the first hymn named Dr. Towner relates in Mr. Sankey's "Story of Gospel Hymns":

"Some years ago Mr. Sankey was conducting a series of meetings in Brockton, Massachusetts, and I had the pleasure of singing for him. One night a young man rose in a testimony meeting and said, 'I am not quite sure—but I am going to trust and obey.' I jotted down that sentence and sent it with the little story to the Reverend J. H. Sammis, a Presbyterian minister. He wrote the hymn and the tune was born."

As a composer of music for evangelistic purposes Dr. Towner occupied a prominent place among writers. He was a very able leader of choirs and of large assemblies and an impressive singer, pos-

lost one of its most prominent figures. No man in the history of modern sacred song possessed the combination of leader, singer, writer and publisher to the degree of success as did Mr. E. O. Excell, or stood higher in the estimation of his contemporaries. He had a marvelous voice range, extending from low C to G above, and of a quality and power seldom heard. As a leader he was the peer of any one in the field during the years of his activities.

I met him for the first time in San Francisco in 1889, when he was with Sam Jones conducting a series of meetings.

Of his hymns that have become known around the world, and everywhere loved, may be mentioned the following: "Let Him In," "God Calling Yet," "Scatter Sunshine," "Count Your Blessings, "Since I Have Been Redeemed," etc.

His father, the Reverend J. J. Excell, was a minister of the German Reformed Church, and a good singer, it is said. Mr. Excell spent some years at the trade of a mason and brick layer, where it may be assumed he acquired his strong physique, which was a notable characteristic of his personality. His passion for music led him out of this work at the age of twenty, when he began teaching country singing schools.

He labored with many of the most famous evangelists and for twenty years was associated with the Reverend Sam Jones. His last work was with Gipsy Smith in Louisville, Kentucky—in the midst of which he was obliged to stop his labor and return home. After more than thirty weeks in Wesley Hospital he answered the call of the Great Reaper, June 10, 1921. He was born in Stark County, Ohio, December 13, 1851.

It is interesting at this point to call attention to the fact that Chicago has been the home, at some period of their lives, of more celebrated writers, singers and leaders of evangelistic song than any other city in the world. If we should call the roll and they should stand before us, we would see such men as Dr. Root, Dr. Palmer, Dr. Towner, P. P. Bliss, Ira D. Sankey, E. O. Excell, T. M. Towne, Charles M. Alexander and others, each of whom has left his mark on his day and generation that the passing of years will not erase.

Then, if we were to add the names of those still living, all of whom have earned the right to stand with those gifted men, one would be still more surprised. That great city might well be thankful that such a number of distinguished men have lived and wrought within her borders, for it is such men,

LET HIM IN

REV. J. B. ATCHINSON

E. O. EXCELL

1. There's a stran-ger at the door, Let him in,
2. O-pen now to him your heart, Let him in,
3. Hear you now his lov - ing voice? Let him in,
4. Now ad - mit the heavenly Guest, Let him in,
Let the Savior in, let the Savior in

He has been there oft be - fore, Let him in:
If you wait he will de - part, Let him in,
Now, oh, now make him your choice, Let him in,
He will make for you a feast, Let him in,
Let the Savior in, let the Savior in,

Let him in ere he is gone, Let him in, the Ho-ly one,
Let him in, He is your Friend, He your soul will sure de-fend,
He is stand-ing at the door, Joy to you he will re - store,
He will speak your sins for-given, And when earth ties all are riven,

Je-sus Christ, the Father's Son, Let him in.
He will keep you to the end, Let him in.
And his name you will a-dore, Let him in.
He will take you home to heav'n, Let him in.
Let the Savior in, let the Savior in.

with their compeers, that are the vital and saving
factors in our cities and nations. Whether the coming generation will add to that number is yet to be
seen.

Major D. W. Whittle

Among the most prominent and successful
authors of hymns that were used in the evangelistic
movements of the last two generations, Major
Whittle, who wrote for the most part under the
name of "El Nathan," stands well in the front
rank. He began writing in 1877, and from that
time on for many years wrote extensively and
almost entirely for Mr. McGranahan, with whom
he was associated in his evangelistic work. His
hymns soon became recognized as among the best
in use in those times and were in great favor
everywhere.

His writings are characterized by faithfulness to
Scriptural teaching, and emphasis on the cardinal
doctrines, among which are the following:

"I Know Whom I Have Believed," "Moment
by Moment," "I Shall Be Satisfied," "The
Crowning Day Is Coming," "I'll Stand By You
Till the Morning," and "No More the Curse."

The Major made no claim to being a poet, but there are in his hymns evidences that he possessed poetic gifts. A notable example of this is to be found in some verses written on the death, by accident, of an only son.

I was assisting him in a series of meetings in Pennsylvania, in 1894, when he received the news of his son's death. He hastened to his family to be with them in paying the last tribute of love to the son, and then returned to continue the work from which he was called.

Shortly afterward he wrote the verses which are worthy to be quoted here, not only as showing his poetic trend of mind, but his patient submission to the will of God, which was ever a characteristic of his.

> "Be still, my heart! Thy Savior knows full well
>   The burden on thee laid;
> And to thy side He comes, with love to heal
>   The wound His love hath made.
> Close by the sheep, in paths of darkness led,
>   He walks, the Shepherd true;
> 'I will not leave you comfortless,' He said,
>   'I will come unto you.'
>
> "No love but His can fill the vacant place
>   And soothe the bitter pain:
> No power but His can send the needed grace,
>   To count thy sorrow's gain:

No hand but His can wipe the falling tear,
    For He on earth hath wept;
No voice but His can at the grave give cheer,
    For there He once hath slept.

"And still He weeps with all His own who weep,
    Our great High Priest above;
And through their night of woe He still doth keep
    His silent watch of love.
He feels each sigh, each throb of aching head,
    And whispers soft and low,
'I will not leave you comfortless and sad,
    I will come unto you.'"

These verses were soon set to beautiful music by his daughter, May Whittle (Mrs. W. R. Moody).

As a hymn it has not the elements required to win popular favor or to render it useful for congregational purposes, but it has been used by soloists with wonderful effect.

Another poem, the last he ever wrote, was written or composed during a night made sleepless by pain, and was suggested by the chimes of a clock in his room. As it will be interesting to read his last message, it is given. It will be seen that his mind was still clear, his heart true and his hope bright, as he looked forward to soon being in the presence of his Lord.

"Swift with melodious feet, the midnight hours pass by;
    As with each passing bell so sweet, I think, 'My Lord
    draws nigh.'

I see heaven's open door, I hear God's gracious voice;
I see the blood-washed round the throne, and with them
I rejoice.

"It may be that these sounds are the golden bells so sweet,
Which tell me of the near approach of the heav'nly High
Priest's feet.
Not every night is thus; some nights with pain are drear;
Then I join my moan with creation's groan, and the
chimes I do not hear.

"But the Lord remains the same; faithful He must abide;
And on His Word my soul will rest, for He is by my side.
Some midnight, sleepless saints, made quick by pain to hear,
Shall join the glad and welcome cry, 'The Bridegroom
draweth near.'

"Then I shall see His face, His beauteous image bear;
I'll know His love and wondrous grace, and in His glory
share.
So sing my soul in praise, as bells chime o'er and o'er,
The coming of the Lord draws near, when time shall be
no more."

Major Whittle was born in Chicopee Falls,
Massachusetts, November 22, 1840, and was christened Daniel Webster Whittle. Sometime in the
fifties he went to Chicago, and in time became associated with Wells, Fargo and Co., and later the
cashier of its bank. In 1861 at the outbreak of the
Civil War he enlisted in the 72nd Illinois Infantry
and became 2nd lieutenant of Company B.

He served through the war and was at one time
Provost Marshal on the staff of Gen. O. O. Howard, who was ever after his life-long friend. He
was with Sherman on his march to the sea. He
was sent home wounded from Vicksburg, having
been shot in the arm while leading a charge for his
wounded Captain, and at the close of the war was
breveted "Major," the title by which he was known
thereafter. While at home he met, for the first
time, Mr. Moody, who became a true and devoted
friend to the last. The occasion of their meeting
was—as told by himself:

"A big meeting of some kind was being held in
the Tabernacle, and with some help I was able to
attend, although I was still weak from loss of
blood and with my arm in a sling. I was called
upon to speak, and as I got slowly to my feet,
feeling shy and embarrassed, a strong voice called
out, 'Give him three cheers, boys!' and they were
given with a will, for every heart was bursting with
patriotism in those days, and the sight of a wounded
soldier in a blue uniform stirred the blood. And
how that kindly thought and the ringing cheer
stirred my heart, too! How grateful I was to them
and to the one who called out, 'Give him three
cheers,' and for what his friendship meant to me

from that moment onward; stimulating, encouraging, appreciating in a twinkling the whole situation —the young soldier's embarrassment—his need of a friendly word of help!"

After the war closed, the Major became connected with the Elgin Watch Co., and for some years was its treasurer, which position he held at the time he entered evangelistic work in 1873, due to Mr. Moody's influence, though it should be said, it soon became very evident that his decision was also in obedience to the call from the Lord, for his labors were greatly owned of God from the very beginning.

I became acquainted with him in 1870. We were living not far apart on the west side of Chicago, and occasionally met, as did our families. He was at that time the superintendent of one of the largest mission Sunday Schools in the city, which was located on that side, and I recall singing for him on one or more occasions, and also of assisting him in a series of meetings he was conducting in one of the nearby towns. I thus came to know and to value him highly in those earlier years.

Twenty years later when Mr. McGranahan's health gave out, necessitating his retiring permanently from all public activities, I became associated with the Major and assisted him thereafter in the most of his evangelistic work for the remainder of his life, both at home and abroad.

The last work Major Whittle did was among the soldiers in camp, during the Spanish-American War. He cherished the memories of his army life many years before, and he loved men, hence it was impossible for him to refrain from devoting his time and strength to the boys called to arms.

That he might be of the greatest service to them, he went into camp, ate with them, slept with them and lived the life they were living, and devoted his strength to their physical and spiritual welfare without thought of himself. In so doing, however, he undermined his strength to such an extent that he came home broken in health, from which he never recovered, and from that time on for the three years he lived his strength gradually failed till the last year or more he was confined to his room and bed.

His home for some years had been in Northfield, but for the last year or two of his life he lived with his daughter, Mrs. Moody. My last visit with him was some months before he died. It was during the August conference in the summer of 1900. When sitting by his bedside, he said to me: "What

is the last hymn you have written?" I replied that
I had just completed the music to a hymn entitled,
"O House of Many Mansions." Said he, "I wish
you would sing it for me—I would like to pray
that it may be greatly blessed of God." I did so,
the first verse of which is as follows:

"O House of many Mansions,
    Thy doors are open wide,
And dear are all the faces
    Upon the other side.
Thy portals they are golden,
    And those who enter in
Shall know no more of sorrow,
    Of weariness and sin."

How well his prayers have been answered may
never be known, but the hymn was for years a favorite with congregations, and it has been used by
evangelistic singers as a solo.

Major Whittle loved children and had a happy
faculty of presenting the great truths of the Gospel in such a way as to make it attractive and
easily understood by them. It was his custom
wherever he was conducting meetings, to hold special services for them; and in order to make these
services attractive he gave blackboard illustrations
and chemical experiments to make the truths

plain. So successful was he in these services that there was a demand for his addresses, and to supply this demand they were published in book form.

Few men were ever more sincerely respected and loved than was Major Whittle, and none more deservingly; nor has it been my privilege to know a more manly, self-sacrificing Christian man, or one whose sincerity and loyalty to his Lord more surely had their springs in the depths of his heart.

When his life-long friend, Mr. Moody, passed away, he bemoaned the fact that he could not have been taken and Mr. Moody spared to continue his great work. The year and eight months that remained for him to suffer were not lost, however, for he spent many of his days and nights in prayer for his large circle of friends, naming them one by one before the Lord, and for the objects that claimed his thought and interest. Not many men have had such a hold on God in prayer as had he.

Major Whittle passed on to be with his Lord at his daughter's home in Northfield, March 4, 1901.

It can be truthfully said of him that "for him to live was Christ," and that his work, both in the hymns he wrote and in the sermons he preached during his life as an evangelist, "was wrought in God."

FANNY J. CROSBY

There is no character in the history of American Sunday School and evangelistic hymns so outstanding as that of Fanny Crosby, and it is quite as true that more of her hymns than of any other writer of the nineteenth century have found an abiding place in the hearts of Christians, the world over. So evident is this that there is a fragrance about her very name that no other has.

Miss Crosby was born in New York, in Putnam County, March 24, 1820, and when but six weeks of age lost her sight through improper treatment, which rendered her blind for the remainder of her life.

At the age of 15 she was placed in the New York Institute for the Blind, where she was educated, and became a member of the faculty, having assigned to her the teaching of history and rhetoric.

During the years she was thus engaged, she had the opportunity of meeting some of the famous men in American history; among whom were Presidents Van Buren, Tyler and Cleveland, the latter being connected with the institution.

Fanny Crosby's talent for poetic expression was early manifested and early recognized by Mr.

Bradbury, Dr. Root and Drs. Lowry and Doane, as well as others among the musicians of those years, all of whom took advantage of it in the beginning of their careers as composers. She was four years younger than Mr. Bradbury and born in the same year as Dr. Root, hence was contemporary with the early writers of Sunday School music, for whom she wrote extensively.

She also wrote verses for a number of Dr. Root's popular secular songs and cantatas; but her first hymn was written for Mr. Bradbury, of which the first two lines are as follows:

> "We are going, we are going
> To a land beyond the tide."

This was followed by many others, but her first hymn to attain universal favor was, "Safe in the Arms of Jesus," already referred to. Of this beautiful hymn, Dr. John Hall, long famous as pastor of the Fifth Avenue Presbyterian Church of New York City, once said at a great Sunday School convention, "It gives more comfort and satisfaction to mothers who have lost children than any other hymn I have ever known."

In the years that intervened between then and the close of her remarkable career she wrote over eight thousand hymns, according to Hubert P. Main, who kept a record of them, many of which have long been favorites the world around and have been translated into many languages.

A few only, besides those already mentioned, may be noted: "The Bright Forever," "Pass Me Not, O Gentle Savior," "I Am Thine, O Lord," "Hold Thou My Hand," "Jesus Is Calling," "Blessed Assurance," "Nearer the Cross," "Savior, More Than Life to Me," "Jesus, Keep Me Near the Cross," and "Saved by Grace."

A very touching incident occurred while the last named was being sung at the anniversary of Fanny's 93rd birthday in Bridgeport, Conn., where she spent the later years of her life.

A few months previous to this she was a guest in my home in Brooklyn, and while there met and heard a very delightful young lady friend sing, who, like herself, had been blind from childhood. Wishing to have us both present to aid in the cele-bration of her birthday, she wrote asking that I come and take part in the service and bring the blind singer with me. I did so, and when we ar-rived there found it was arranged that after the opening service, which was held in the Methodist church of which Fanny was a member, I should take charge, relate the history of some of her hymns, and have the blind friend sing.

Fanny made a ten-minute address in a voice that could be heard by all, frail though she was, that touched the hearts of her friends. The singing, personality, and beautiful voice of the blind girl also made a deep impression.

The service increased in interest until the last number was reached, which was "Saved by Grace." This had been reserved for the close, with the intention of having the congregation join in the singing of it. The history of the hymn, as well as some incidents of interest connected with it, were related, and the congregation invited to join in the chorus, as the verses were to be sung. Fanny was seated behind the blind singer on the pulpit platform, and when the last verse was about to be sung, she stepped to the singer's side and put an arm about her as she sang—

"Some day; till then I'll watch and wait
My lamp all trimmed and burning bright,
That when my Savior ope's the gate,
My soul to Him may take its flight."

It was a tense moment and a scene never to be forgotten, to see the two blind singers standing side by side, the one beautiful and fair in her youth, and the other beautiful, though bent under the weight of many years, whose feet were already on the portals of the door through which she would soon enter into the presence of Him whom she had so long sung.

Mention has been made in the sketch of Dr. Doane of the circumstances of her writing for him "Safe in the Arms of Jesus," which, with the incident (which follows) of her composing a hymn at my request, will serve to illustrate how responsive she was, and how ever ready her talent to be at the service of others.

For a good many years she lived in Brooklyn where she was available for help in work upon hymns. I had occasion to call on Mr. Sankey one day at his home in Brooklyn and found her there. I said to her: "Fanny, I have a subject for a hymn, and I would like you to write some verses for me." "Good," she said; "what is it?" "Eye Hath Not Seen, Ear Hath Not Heard," I said. "Good!" she again exclaimed. I then told her that it had occurred to me that the verse of Scripture I had quoted to her would make a good chorus, and indeed I had already some music for it in mind, and

I would be glad if she would give me some verses suitable for it.

As she never composed without a small book or Testament, held open before her eyes, she was given one and retired to an adjoining room. Returning in a short time, she repeated to me the first verse that came to her, which reads—

> "They tell me of a land so fair,
>   Unseen by mortal eyes,
> Where spring in fadeless beauty blooms,
>   Beneath unclouded skies."

"Splendid, Fanny," I said; "give me some more like it." She retired again and soon returned with the second beautiful verse—

> "They tell me of a land so fair,
>   Where all is light and song,
> Where angel choirs their anthems join
>   With yonder blood-washed throng."

I repeated my exclamation and asked for more, when she again retired and soon came back with a still more beautiful verse—

> "No radiant beams from sun or moon
>   Adorn that land so fair,
> For He Who sits upon the throne
>   Shines forth resplendent there."

Then came the last verse so expressive of her joyous and ever hopeful nature—

"O land of light and love and joy,
  Where comes no night of care,
What will our song of triumph be
  When we shall enter there!"

While her hymn never attained "popular favor," so-called, it has been very much used and has been a blessing to many.

I may say in passing that this hymn was the last I had the privilege, with Mrs. Stebbins joining me, to sing for Mr. Moody at the last service he held in Northfield, shortly before he began what proved to be his last series of meetings, in Kansas City.

There was probably no writer in her day who appealed more to the varied experiences of the Christian life or who expressed more sympathetically the deep longings of the human heart than Fanny Crosby. She had been tried in the furnace of affliction and knew by long experience how to interpret the heart's desires. She possessed, to a marked degree, a joyous as well as a sympathetic nature, which made her kin to youth to the very end of life; no one could laugh more heartily or weep more sincerely, so responsive was she to every experience in life. These traits can be read between the lines of many of her hymns; for unquestioning faith in God's love and His Word, deep spirituality and abounding hope pervaded all her writings.

Hence, the passing of this blind singer was but stepping from the darkened room in which she dwelt into the unshaded glory of the upper world —where her heart had long been.

Fanny Crosby died at her home in Bridgeport, February 12, 1915, and it was my privilege to attend the funeral services. A vast throng, too great by many hundreds to get into the church, came to pay the last tribute of respect and honor to one who had been such a blessing to the great host of the Lord's people in every land.

What must have been her surprise when her eyes, so long closed to the light of this fair world, suddenly opened to behold the face of Him whom she had loved with a joyous devotion all through the years of her long life and upon the faces of loved ones her eyes had never seen!

WILLIAM F. SHERWIN

I had the pleasure of knowing Mr. Sherwin well during the earlier years of my activities in the evangelistic field, and have always counted it one of the happy events of those days.

We first met in Boston in the spring of 1876, where he conducted the singing for a Sunday School convention, held in Tremont Temple, with which I was connected.

I remember well his singing very effectively and artistically the old classic among sacred songs, "Flee As a Bird to Your Mountain." His manner of rendering and his well trained and sympathetic voice made a lasting impression upon me.

Our next meeting was some months afterward at a Sunday School Parliament held at the Thousand Islands in the summer of 1877, conducted by the Reverend Wilbur F. Crafts, of which Mr. Sherwin was one of the teachers. I had charge of the music.

The incident that fixed this occasion in my mind was the rendering of the beautiful hymn, "Hallelujah, What a Savior!" which I sang at one of the sessions. He came to me at the close with evi-

DAY IS DYING IN THE WEST

MARY A. LATHBURY   WILLIAM F. SHERWIN

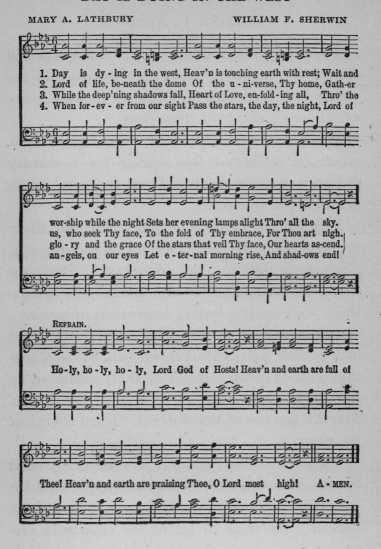

1. Day   is dy - ing in the west, Heav'n is touching earth with rest; Wait and
2. Lord of life, be-neath the dome Of the u - ni-verse, Thy home, Gath-er
3. While the deep'ning shadows fall, Heart of Love, en-fold - ing all,   Thro' the
4. When for - ev - er from our sight Pass the stars, the day, the night, Lord of

wor-ship while the night Sets her evening lamps alight Thro' all the sky.
us, who seek Thy face, To the fold of Thy embrace, For Thou art nigh.
glo - ry and the grace Of the stars that veil Thy face, Our hearts as-cend.
an - gels, on our eyes Let e - ter-nal morning rise, And shad-ows end!

REFRAIN.

Ho - ly, ho - ly, ho - ly, Lord God of Hosts! Heav'n and earth are full of

Thee! Heav'n and earth are praising Thee, O Lord most high!   A - MEN.

dences of being greatly affected by it, not so much by my rendering, but because of the new setting of the great truth of the atonement Mr. Bliss had made. The hymn was comparatively little known at that time, which had much to do with the impression it made. It seemed to be a coincidence that the first time I had the pleasure of hearing Mr. Sherwin sing I was impressed by the song, and the first time he heard me, he was impressed by my song—quite a fair exchange of compliments.

Our subsequent meetings were either at Sunday School conventions where he was one of the speakers, or in New York, which was for many years his headquarters.

Mr. Sherwin was a talented musician of recognized ability, though his work in that profession was rather out of the beaten track, as his interest in Sunday School work and his efficiency as a speaker and teacher on lines of Sunday School methods absorbed a good deal of his time and interest. He was for some time musical editor for the Century Company, and also connected with Bigelow & Main.

In the early history of the Chautauqua movement, Mr. Sherwin was associated with Dr. Vincent in that work, having charge of the musical department, in which he proved his efficiency and usefulness in a marked degree.

His best known hymns are: "Day Is Dying in the West," "Break Thou the Bread of Life," "Beautiful Valley of Eden," "Sound the Battle Cry," and "Hear the Call."

The two latter stirring hymns were written by him, both words and music. "Beautiful Valley of Eden" was also very popular in the seventies and eighties; and is yet a great favorite among the older singers. But the two settings to Miss Lathbury's beautiful hymns did not come into prominence until some time later, and by their merit in both words and music are destined to a permanent place in hymnology. There are few, if any, more useful and beautiful evening hymns than "Day Is Dying in the West." That hymn and "Break Thou the Bread of Life" were written for and copyrighted by Dr. Vincent in 1877, while Mr. Sherwin was associated with him in his Chautauqua work.

Mr. Sherwin was born March 14, 1826, and died April 14, 1888, honored for the distinguished service he had rendered the great cause he loved and served for many years.

John R. Sweney

I did not have the privilege of an extended acquaintance with Mr. Sweney, but the singing of his songs for many years gave me a feeling of comradeship.

His contribution to Sunday School music placed him among the most prominent and successful composers of that class of music.

His career as a musician began, practically, when he entered the army as leader of a military band during the Civil War. On his return from the service he was made Professor of Music at the Pennsylvania Military Academy, located at West Chester, his home town, a position he filled for nearly thirty years.

His compositions, prior to 1871, were largely of a secular nature and for various purposes; but from that time he devoted his talent to the production of sacred music.

It is said that he was the editor, or associate editor, of sixty song books, and his name with that of William J. Kirkpatrick so often appeared that "Sweney and Kirkpatrick" became a trade-mark for excellence.

Mr. Sweney was a popular leader at conventions

and camp meetings, and the many thousands who spent their summers at Ocean Grove gave testimony to his ability.

Of his many hymns that attained popular favor, the best known are: "Beulah Land," "On Calvary's Brow," "More About Jesus," and "There Is Sunshine in My Soul."

Mr. Sweney's music has the stamp of originality and the marks of the musician in that he possessed the faculty of producing music adapted to the sentiment of his text, for which reason many of his songs will live as monuments to his memory.

During the years of his connection with the Military Academy at West Chester, he was honored with the degree of Doctor of Music.

Mr. Sweney was born at West Chester, Pennsylvania, December 31, 1837, and passed away at his home in the same city April 10, 1899.

William J. Kirkpatrick

The songs of Mr. Kirkpatrick I have known, loved and sung for two score and more years. I came in touch with him through correspondence, but our paths never crossed until he came to Northfield with Dr. Doane. Some years

SUNSHINE IN THE SOUL

E. E. HEWITT   JNO. R. SWENEY

1. There's sun-shine in my soul to-day, More glo - ri - ous and bright
2. There's mu - sic in my soul to-day, A car - ol to the King,
3. There's spring-time in my soul to-day, For, when the Lord is near,
4. There's glad-ness in my soul to-day, And hope, and praise, and love,

Than glows in an - y earth-ly skies, For Je - sus is my light.
And Je - sus, lis - ten-ing, can hear The songs I can - not sing.
The dove of peace sings in my heart, The flow'rs of grace ap - pear.
For bless-ings which He gives me now, For joys "laid up" a - bove.

REFRAIN.

O there's sun - - - shine, bless - ed sun - - shine,
O there's sun - shine in the soul, bless - ed sun-shine in the soul,

When the peace - ful, hap - py mo-ments roll;
hap - py mo - ments roll;

When Je - sus shows His smil - ing face, There is sun-shine in the soul.

WILLIAM J. KIRKPATRICK

HOMER RODEHEAVER

later, accompanied by Mrs. Kirkpatrick, he spent
portions of several summers in that pleasant re-
treat, which afforded me the opportunity of knowing him more intimately and the privilege of
delightful conversations on subjects of mutual
interest. We also worked together in conducting
services of songs in the parlors of the hotel. During those pleasant and memorable days I was able
to catch the spirit of the man and discover some of
the elements of his power as a writer, and I count
it an honor, as it has been a pleasure, to have
had personal contact with so great and gifted a
writer of songs which are sung wherever the gospel
is preached.

Mr. Kirkpatrick was born in Ireland, February
27, 1838, but at an early age came with his parents
to the United States and settled in Pennsylvania.
His father was a musician, hence he came naturally
by his love and talent for music. He was for years
director of music in Grace M. E. Church, Philadelphia, and organist and choirmaster many years
in the Ebenezer Church of the same city. He
studied voice, theory and harmony under prominent
teachers; this, with a practical experience in church
and Sunday School work, constituted a rare equip-

ment for his life work. In connection with his composition he devoted much time to the conducting of music in conventions and camp meetings.

His first collection of songs was published in 1859 and was entitled "Devotional Melodies." He served as fife major of the 91st Regiment, Pennsylvania Volunteers, under Colonel E. M. Gregory, in the Civil War, but was returned to Philadelphia and assigned to work as a ship builder.

In 1866 his second book, "Heart and Voice," was published. It was a large book and contained every hymn in the Methodist Episcopal hymn book, with many original selections. It was, probably, the second hymn and tune book issued in the United States. Some of his most notable songs were first printed in this book, among them "Saved to the Uttermost," "Wait, and Murmur Not," "Resting at the Cross," and "Companionship with Jesus."

In 1880 he became associated with Mr. John R. Sweney in compiling song books, the number of which—during the next seventeen years—is said to be fifty volumes. At the end of that period he retired from most of his public activities and devoted the rest of his life to composition and editing.

JESUS SAVES

PRISCILLA J. OWENS   WM. J. KIRKPATRICK

1. We have heard a joy - ful sound, Je - sus saves, Je - sus saves;
2. Waft it on the roll - ing tide, Je - sus saves, Je - sus saves;
3. Sing a - bove the bat - tle's strife, Je - sus saves, Je - sus saves;
4. Give the winds a might - y voice, Je - sus saves, Je - sus saves;

Spread the glad - ness all a - round, Je - sus saves, Je - sus saves;
Tell to sin - ners far and wide, Je - sus saves, Je - sus saves;
By His death and end - less life, Je - sus saves, Je - sus saves;
Let the na - tions now re - joice, Je - sus saves, Je - sus saves:

Bear the news to ev - 'ry land, Climb the steeps and cross the waves,
Sing, ye is - lands of the sea, Ech - o back, ye o - cean caves,
Sing it soft - ly thro' the gloom, When the heart for mer - cy craves,
Shout sal - va - tion full and free, High - est hill and deep - est caves,

On - ward, 'tis our Lord's com - mand, Je - sus saves, Je - sus saves.
Earth shall keep her Ju - bi - lee, Je - sus saves, Je - sus saves.
Sing in tri - umph o'er the tomb, Je - sus saves, Je - sus saves.
This our song of vic - to - ry, Je - sus saves, Je - sus saves.

Used by permission of Hope Pub. Co., owners.

Among the hymns that have made his name known in every part of the world are: "Wait, and Murmur Not," "Jesus Saves," "Blessed Be the Name," "I'm Coming Home," "He Hideth My Soul," " 'Tis So Sweet" and "When Love Shines In."

Mr. Kirkpatrick died suddenly, at his residence in Germantown, Philadelphia. Mrs. Kirkpatrick found her husband sitting in his favorite chair fast asleep—as she supposed—about four o'clock on the morning of September 29, 1921. On the floor at his feet was found a manuscript bearing the notation—"9-29, 2 A.M."—which would indicate that he had heard his Master's call while yet in the midst of his last prayer, or doubtless he would have written a third stanza.

"Just as Thou wilt, Lord, this is my cry:
Just as Thou wilt, to live or to die.
I am Thy servant; Thou knowest best;
Just as Thou wilt, Lord, labor or rest.

"Just as Thou wilt, Lord,—which shall it be,
Life everlasting waiting for me,
Or shall I tarry here at Thy feet?
Just as Thou wilt, Lord, whate'er is meet."

To voice such words of resignation, then close his eyes on earth to open them—in a moment's time—in the presence of his Lord, is as striking and impressive as it is beautiful. What a glorious awakening his must have been! Well might every child of God covet a similar ending to labor, turmoil and dying for that rest, peace and life eternal that awaits the faithful servant of the King of all kings.

Hubert P. Main

These reminiscences have thus far been confined to writers who have passed on to their reward; I should like, however, to pay a passing tribute to one still living (1924), who has enriched my life by his cordial friendship and kindly regard for more than two score years, and who is the only one left of the distinguished company of the earlier writers of my acquaintance. I refer to Mr. Hubert P. Main, composer of popular Sunday School music in Mr. Bradbury's time, and of evangelistic music in later years.

For sixty years he was connected with the Bigelow & Main publishing house, and not until that company went out of business did he retire to quiet life. It is probable that he has edited or assisted in editing more hymn books than any other man

WE SHALL MEET, BY AND BY

JOHN ATKINSON

HUBERT P. MAIN

1. We shall meet be-yond the riv-er, By and by, by and by; And the darkness
2. We shall strike the harps of glo-ry, By and by, by and by; We shall sing re-
3. We shall see and be like Je-sus, By and by, by and by; Who a crown of
4. There our tears shall all cease flowing, By and by, by and by; And with sweetest

shall be o-ver, By and by, by and by; With the toil-some jour-ney done,
demption's sto-ry, By and by, by and by; And the strains for ev-er-more
life will give us, By and by, by and by; And the an-gels who ful-fil
rap-ture knowing, By and by, by and by; All the blest ones, who have gone

And the glor-ious bat-tle won, We shall shine forth as the sun, By and by, by and by.
Shall resound in sweetness o'er Yonder ev-er-last-ing shore, By and by, by and by.
All the mandates of His will Shall attend, and love us still, By and by, by and by.
To the land of life and song,— We with shoutings shall rejoin, By and by, by and by.

in the history of this class of music. He is an expert in all branches of it, and is considered authority in the history of American church and Sunday School hymnology. Of song and hymn books of all classes he possesses the largest collection, to be found in this country—certainly in any private library, or, quite possibly, in the world. It consists of over seven thousand volumes, nearly one-half of which forms what is known as the "Main Collection" in the Chicago Public Library.

Among his songs that have been a blessing the world over will be found his setting to Fanny Crosby's beautiful words, "Hold Thou My Hand," known and loved everywhere; also the hymn Mr. Sankey used so much and sang with great effect, entitled, "We Shall Meet Beyond the River." "The Bright Forever" and "In the Fadeless Springtime" were great favorites in Sunday Schools half a century ago.

Mr. Main has passed more than eighty milestones in life's journey, but the merry twinkle in his keen eye still remains, and the play of humor that always characterized him has lost little of its charm by the passing of years.

Like ships that pass in the night, we hail him on

his voyage to the land beyond the sea and sing once again, "We Shall Meet Beyond the River, By and By."

CHARLES M. ALEXANDER

Although he does not come under the head of those considered in these sketches, the series would be incomplete did I not make mention of Charles M. Alexander. He was not a composer of music, nor did he essay the rôle of singer, at least in the more important period of his public activities. He was, however, one of the most magnetic and successful leaders of Gospel song in the history of modern evangelism, and it is quite within the truth to say that no other man has had so great an influence upon the world at large, in his sphere of labors, taking into account its world-wide sweep. In girdling the earth twice on evangelistic missions he left a trail of song unequaled for good in the lands he visited.

Our acquaintance began when he was a student at the Moody Bible Institute back in the 1890's. It was during the World's Fair that, with several other evangelists and singers, I was assisting Mr. Moody in a six months' evangelistic campaign in

Chicago. His assistants were given accommodations in the men's department, which was then a dormitory, dining room, class room and office combined. It was not long after my arrival there that Mr. Alexander found his way to my room and made himself known, suggesting that I assist him in the use of his voice and in the interpretation of hymns, as he intended to enter the field as a singer of the Gospel. This I took pleasure in doing, and opportunities to study his character and spirituality were thereby frequently presented. It is needless to say that I was attracted to him, as were all with whom he came in contact. He always went about with a smiling face, a cheering word and a merry laugh, apparently the happiest of all the students in the Institute. He little realized the great talent, latent in him, waiting the time when God would call it forth; and certainly none of his friends saw any evidence of his possessing it at that time—he being just one of two or three hundred students there to get an equipment for service in some part of the Lord's vineyard.

In the course of time he went out into the evangelistic field with M. B. Williams to begin his life work. Occasionally he sent a copy of some local paper containing an account of the work in which he was engaged, thus keeping me in touch with him for some years. His awakening to the fact that he possessed the gifts that made him famous did not obtain for some years, and not till he joined Dr. Torrey in Australia on his tour around the world did his wonderful powers of leadership burst upon the horizon full orbed. From that time on his sun seemed ever to be at its zenith, for there was never evidence that his powers were waning, but rather gaining to the last.

Back of a personal attractiveness and charm of manner that few possess, there was a love for the salvation of souls and the determination, both in public appeal and personal contact, to lose no opportunity to win men to his Lord.

Mr. Alexander never seemed to be at a loss to know what to do, no matter what the circumstances. One incident, as amusing as it was interesting, will illustrate his ability to meet emergencies and turn defeat into victory.

Some years ago I was assisting one of the New York pastors in a series of Sunday evening services, which were being held in a well-known theater.

Just before the sermon, one evening, a note was handed to me saying that Mr. Alexander was in the audience. I handed it to the pastor, who decided it best to go on with his sermon and to call for Mr. Alexander at the close, which he did. After some persuasion, Mr. Alexander came down from the topmost gallery, accompanied by his pianist, and sang the chorus of "He Will Hold Me Fast," until the audience had learned it. He then announced that he would present a copy of the song to any one who would stand up and sing it correctly. A colored man rose in the body of the house and sang it perfectly, after which Alexander said: "Good, my man, are you a Christian?" "Yes, Sah," responded the negro, "an' mah name's Charles Alexander—an' ahm from Tennes-see, too!" My first thought, after the laughter ceased, was, "How will Charlie meet such an unexpected situation?" He lost no time, however, in saying to the man, "Come down here; I want to shake hands with you." The man walked down to the footlights and Mr. Alexander reached over, took him by the hand and assured him he was glad to meet him; he then requested the fellow to face the audience and offered prayer, which restored the thought of the congregation to the serious subject that had engaged their attention during the evening.

It will be of interest to know that the last cam-

paign Mr. Alexander was engaged in was at
Detroit, the winter before he passed away. He
was assisting one of the largest churches of
that city in a series of meetings that continued
many weeks and resulted in hundreds of conversions.

For several years Mr. Alexander either assisted
in the conduct of the music at the general conference at Northfield or had full charge, as was the
case in later years. He was for the most of that
time given one hour in the morning of each day
during the conference for a service of song. The
sessions were always varied with hymns by the
congregation, songs by the children's choir, solos,
duets and quartets, and by incidents, of which he
seemed to have an inexhaustible supply to relate
just when most appropriate. He had the congregation always on the tiptoe of expectation, as he
never lacked for something which appealed to them.

Those services were attractive to young and old
alike, and always attended with blessing. The
memory of his untiring efforts to win men to his
Savior can never be effaced.

Mr. Alexander was born at Meadow, Tennes-
see, October 24, 1867, and died October 13, 1920,
at his home in Birmingham, England.

Mention has been made of the number of singers and writers of Gospel songs who at one time in their career made Chicago their home. In this connection it is interesting to note another remarkable fact: that a group of six men mentioned in these sketches, all of whom were noted singers as well as writers, and indeed quite the first to become known as "Singing Evangelists," were born within an area of probably not more than five or six hundred miles. The largest number came from the State of Pennsylvania, among whom were Ira D. Sankey, P. P. Bliss, D. B. Towner, James McGranahan and C. C. Case. E. O. Excell was from Ohio; Philip Phillips (who was the forerunner of the large army of singers of the gospel) was born in New York. Then if Dr. Palmer, Dr. Sweney, and Dr. Lowry were to be counted (Dr. Palmer in New York, and Drs. Sweney and Lowry in Pennsylvania) it makes a list extraordinary and remarkable for the men who compose it, they being among the most noteworthy in the history of evangelistic song.

It may have been a mere coincidence that such a large number of those first to enter that great field should have come from the heart of the Eastern States, and yet God may have had a purpose in it. There can be no question, however, but that He set the seal of His approval to their ministry.

Mrs. George C. Stebbins

In these pages occasional mention has been made of Mrs. Stebbins, and I desire to offer a grateful tribute to her memory by declaring that no account of my public activities would be complete without placing to her credit much of the good that may have been accomplished.

Endowed with rare intuition and judgment, with grace of mind and heart, a winsome personality, and with a voice that was full, sympathetic and pleasing in quality, all of which she dedicated to the cause to which our lives had been devoted, her ministries to her friends—and above all to her family and home,—are beyond words of mine to appraise.

I desire also to acknowledge my indebtedness to her for a life of nearly half a century of singular happiness and helpfulness in every situation and circumstance during those years.

Elma Miller—for that was the name by which she was known in earlier years,—was one of the fairest among her associates; and it was prophesied by those who knew her that she would be a blessing wherever her lot might be cast. The prophecies were abundantly fulfilled, for she left a trail of blessing wherever she went, in her own land and beyond the seas.

Nor did her kindly ministries cease—even amid her own suffering—until she was suddenly called to join the choir invisible.

The way has been lonely since she left me, but I am content to know that "Weeping may endure for a night, but joy cometh in the morning."

DWIGHT L. MOODY

I met Mr. Moody for the first time in 1871, in Chicago, not many months after I made that city my home. I had seen him occasionally in the meetings he was conducting, and had observed his earnest, forceful way, and that he never seemed to have time for the ordinary conventionalities of life.

One day, as I was looking over some publications in the book store of Fleming H. Revell, a brother-in-law of Mr. Moody, the latter came rushing in and, recognizing me, said, as he hurriedly passed by, "Stebbins, give Revell fifty cents for my Sunday School."

He did his errand and without further word departed as hurriedly as he entered. I was fortunate enough to have just that amount with me, and, of course, handed it to Mr. Revell as readily as if it had been at the command of a king.

Those who knew Mr. Moody intimately, especially in connection with his work, knew how he prosecuted it with all the enthusiasm of his intense nature, and ever with untiring energy, day or night; how he was the life and soul of every effort that was being made to reach the people with the Gospel, and how unceremoniously he would often accost people on the streets and speak to them on the subject nearest his heart; through which acts many who did not know his true spirit or what a remarkable work he had for years been doing among the poor of the city quite misunderstood him.

So whole-heartedly did he give himself not only to that work, but to the Young Men's Christian Association and the Sunday Schools, that it can be truly said there was no man in his time who expended, daily, more mental and physical energy than did he the first fifteen years of his life in Chicago.

The next time I came personally in touch with

him was on the memorable summer afternoon I accompanied Major Whittle to Northfield to spend a Sunday as his guest.

There was no hurried rushing by in our meeting on this occasion, but at least a semblance of the usual formalities in the introduction.

A few weeks prior to this Mr. Moody had finished his first winter's campaign in his own country, after his return from Great Britain, and was resting, apparently care-free after four years of the most strenuous and exacting labors. I found him unaffected toward his neighbors and friends.

Yet, what a contrast! He had but a year before returned from a foreign land the most celebrated and talked-of religious character on either side of the sea, illustrating in a very striking way what God can do in twenty-two years with a youth wholly under His guidance and sway.

At that second meeting I became unexpectedly, but providentially, connected with Moody and Sankey, and from that time on to the end of his career was subject to Mr. Moody's direction in my work.

This enabled me to see a great deal of him, to come into intimate relations with, and to understand some of the secrets of his influence over men.

One of the strongest elements of his character was his determination to succeed in whatever he undertook; indeed, he once said to me that when he first went into his uncle's store in Boston he made up his mind that he would sell more goods than any other one, and it was said that he went out on the street and urged passers-by into the store to make purchases. And while he did not himself tell me so, I afterwards learned that he succeeded in accomplishing his object.

This trait, energized and directed of God in after years, combined with his natural force and the rare judgment with which he was so liberally endowed, was unquestionably one of the secrets of the power which enabled him to become the master of men that he was.

But the greatest gift God bestowed upon him was an abiding love for the welfare and salvation of men, which was given him in the very outset of his Christian life. Those who knew his early history in Christian work, and others who came to know him intimately as the years passed by, saw that such was his master passion, and the motive that actuated him in all the forty-five years of his untiring labors. Everything was secondary to that one object in life. In the founding of the schools at Northfield, and the Bible Institute in Chicago, standing to-day as monuments to his memory more enduring than marble, he had that object only in view, and the mere fitting for usefulness in local communities of all who came to those institutions was secondary.

The giving up of a promising career in business to devote himself to a work he had established among the poor of the city, with no assurance of financial support, firmly relying on the promise of God to supply all his needs, was strong evidence that it was not done in obedience to the call of God alone, but to the added dictates of love for the welfare of mankind that dominated his life.

In the inception of Mr. Moody's brief experience in business, he had set as the goal of his ambition the accumulation of a hundred thousand dollars, which was a great fortune in those days (especially for one of a family of eight children, whose widowed mother fought hard to keep the wolf from the door) and there is no doubt but that he would have accomplished his ambition, for within the year he gave up business—in his early twenties—he had made seven thousand dollars.

But instead of his accumulating a hundred thousand for himself, or a tenth of that amount, it is safe to say that many hundreds of thousands passed through his hands to be used for schools and various Christian enterprises that appealed to him.

He had come in those early years of life to value money only for the good it could do in furthering the cause he so ardently espoused, and therefore the acquisition of wealth for the sake of possessing it or for the use of his family was never a part of his plan.

It will be of interest to the friends of both Moody and Sankey to know that while in England the latter were greatly pained to learn that those who were opposing their work circulated the report that large sums of money were being made from the sale of their hymn book, and that the meetings were really carried on for commercial purposes.

Therefore, when in 1865 "Gospel Hymns" No. 1 was issued, and they began their work in this country, they mutually agreed that neither they nor their families should receive for their own use any royalties accruing from the sale of the book. This agreement was kept to the end of their lives for the sake of the cause in which they engaged.

I have mentioned these facts because of the unkind and ignorant assertions made to the contrary.

Another evidence of Mr. Moody's determination not to give occasion for criticism along this line, was that in all his evangelistic work he would not allow a collection, or "thank-offering," to be taken up for his benefit, nor would he have anything to do with efforts committees might make to raise money to compensate him for his services; neither would he give the slightest intimation as to what would be satisfactory to him, insisting always in leaving that to committees.

The method of compensating evangelists by free-will or thank-offerings that has been in vogue for many years, would seem to be open to less criticism, if properly conducted, than raising money in any other public way, as it gives people the opportunity to express in some substantial manner their appreciation of blessing they may have received. But, doubtless for some good reason, Mr. Moody chose the method he adhered to all through his evangelistic career.

Just a bit of history concerning the make-up of "Gospel Hymns" No. 3. It was necessary that great care should be exercised in the selections of hymns that would conform to Scriptural and evangelistic teaching. The book had been in preparation during the winter of 1887, and the three compilers, Sankey, McGranahan and myself, met at Northfield in the summer of that year, by an arrangement with Mr. Moody, to go over the selections we had to offer. It also occurred to him that, as Major Whittle and Dr. Pentecost, with whom McGranahan and I were associated, would use the books, they might like to pass upon the hymns to be chosen. They were invited, and we became guests of Mr. Moody during those pleasant days.

The mornings were spent in going over the selections that had been made, we three singers singing the songs and the three evangelists sitting in judgment upon them, passing such comments upon their effectiveness and fitness for evangelistic purposes as occurred to them. After the verdict on their merit was pronounced, time would be given to the examination of the hymns as to their strength and to their devotional character as well.

The afternoons would be given up for the most part to relaxations of some sort—to drives, games upon the lawn, etc., and the evenings to social intercourse, always closing the day, as it began, with a chapter from the Word, a song and a prayer.

Mr. Moody entered into the social features of

those memorable days with boyish delight, and into the Christian fellowship over the Word, and the devotional hour both morning and evening, with all the sincerity of his nature. There were some good story-tellers in the company, and they very often gave illustrations of their ability in that direction—usually at the dining table.

There was one day that stands out in my memory when the stories began, one following another, causing roars of laughter that continued until it seemed as if we no longer had strength to endure it. Mr. Sankey went to one side of the room and, with his head on his arms, leaned against the window, and I to another room suffering with pain, each laughing immoderately at the veritable side-splitting incidents that were related.

No one enjoyed the merriment more than Mr. Moody, as no one possessed a keener sense of humor than he, and it always seemed to do him good to relax in that way.

There is often found in villages and towns some one who is looked upon as a "character." This was the case in Northfield.

Mr. Moody told of an amusing conversation he had with a Mr. L., a man he had known all his life and who stuttered noticeably. It was in the summer of 1885, soon after his return from Great Britain, and he was much in demand for services in the small towns about Northfield on Sundays, where large crowds of people came out to hear him.

At that time the main street of Northfield made a little bend at his house, so that the road ran close to his door. One day he was sitting with Sankey on his front porch when Mr. L. came by, driving a span of oxen hitched to a load of black loam. Mr. Moody, knowing he would get some bright reply, called to him: "Mr. L., if you want to do a real benevolent act that will do you good, put that load of loam on my garden back here, for it needs it." Mr. L. replied: "Ye-yes, you and Sa-Sa-Sankey have been havin' some big meetin's round the country." "Yes!" Mr. Moody replied. Mr. L. continued: "If you and Sa-Sa-Sankey would do one thing it would be the bi-bi-biggest day's work you ever did, but you ca-ca-can't do it." "Well, what is it? We would like to know," Mr. Moody queried. "If you would do it one half da-da-day it would turn this town upside down, but you ca-ca-can't do it." Mr. Moody became interested. "Do tell us, for we want to know." To which Mr. L. replied: "If you and Sa-Sa-Sankey would mu-mu-mind your own business!" And with that remark he drove on, leaving them in gales of laughter.

For many years in his dealing with all sorts of people, Mr. Moody had come to be a good judge of men, so it was not difficult for him to recognize at a glance one whose religious life was characterized by pretense and cant. He had had much experience with those who make themselves conspicuous by mannerisms and ways of dress, or who had some peculiar experience they felt called upon to make known, and had found that the best way to deal with such characters was to have as little to do with them as possible.

A good illustration of this occurred during his meetings in Boston in 1877. In a tabernacle that was built for the purpose, off the choir platform was a room put at his disposal for meeting his committees and ushers before service. To avoid interruptions an usher was placed at the door. One day a gentleman called, wishing to see Mr. Moody, and when the usher conveyed the request, he asked, "What sort of a looking man is he?" The usher replied that the man had long hair. Mr. Moody decided at once: "That's enough! Don't you ever let a long-haired man or a short-haired woman in here."

Mr. Moody was intensely human, a great lover of all forms of life, and especially of children. They ever seemed to be his delight, and it was his joy to play with them. This was so characteristic of him that his own children idolized him and would always prefer to be with him than with their young playmates.

It was a great joy to him when his first grand-children—Irene Moody and Emma Fitt—were born. He used to write them letters soon after they came to bless their homes, and when they were old enough to ride about with him he would often be seen with one or the other of them snugly sitting beside him as he drove about the seminary campus and the village.

When little Irene, at four years of age, sickened and died, I can never forget how deeply it affected him, and especially how he manifested his grief when trying to pay a tribute to her at the funeral services.

The child passed away during one of the sum-mer conferences, which proved, by the way, to be the last one he attended, as he was summoned to join little Irene but a few months after she was called away. To accommodate the many friends wishing to attend, the service was held on the lawn

in front of his home. Mr. Moody came out upon
a little balcony over the porch of his house and
poured out his heart in the tribute he struggled
to pay to the child that had entered so much into
his life and had been such a companion to him
during the few brief years of her radiant life.

It was very touching to see the great man sob-
bing out his grief as he tried to tell the people
what a blessing her little life had been to him.

Mr. Moody possessed a very sympathetic nature that was easily influenced by the trials and
sorrows of others; and also the ability to put himself in another's place to a remarkable degree. I
have heard him tell in his sermons of an experience
he had in his early Christian work in Chicago.

Among the poor he was accustomed to visit
there were many who attended no church and who,
through his kindness, became attached to him. The
experience referred to was when he was requested
to conduct the funeral services of one of his Sunday
School children, which he did, although never having been ordained a minister. The child's name
was Emma—that of his only daughter, who was of
about the same age. While he was conducting the
services the thought came to him, "What if that
was my Emma, how would I feel!" The thought

quite overwhelmed him, so really did he put himself in the place of the grief-stricken mother. As he would relate the incident the tears would always come to his eyes, and he seemed, for the time being, to live over the experience.

This gift, in after years, served him in a remarkable way when describing incidents in the lives of some of the great Bible characters. Who can forget his description of Elijah on Mount Carmel, when Elisha prayed that he might have a double portion of his spirit; his dramatic account of Daniel in the lion's den, or his realistic description of the fiery furnace? So real did all these seem to him that his graphic account of them was always thrilling.

Some one wrote in one of his Bibles the following:

> "Ruin by the Fall,
> Redemption by the Blood,
> Regeneration by the Spirit,"

which he chose to call the "Three R's," inasmuch as those three great Scripture truths lay at the foundation of his creed, and he believed them with all the strength of his nature.

It is obvious that no attempt has been made in

these pages to more than mention some of the great work he accomplished among the poor of Chicago, the important service rendered the Young Men's Christian Association in its early history in this country, his work in evangelism, the establishing of the Northfield Schools and the founding of the Bible Institute in Chicago, as it would take volumes to properly describe the good accomplished by these agencies.

So much has already been written and said concerning the great and good man that I have tried to visualize him as I knew him during our twenty-five years of association in the Master's vineyard.

The last public service of Mr. Moody was preaching the gospel of God's love to the world in Kansas City, in the autumn of 1899. While there engaged in what promised to be one of the largest movements in his history (Convention Hall, with its fifteen to twenty thousand seats being filled night after night) the order came to cease pleading with men to be reconciled to God, and to lay down the burden he had borne nearest his heart for the many years of his great activities.

Kind friends accompanied him to his home in Northfield where, surrounded by those most dear to him, he lingered for four weeks with varying hope and despair of recovery and restoration to the work he loved, but his work was done, and the call came for him to depart and be with his Lord.

The funeral services were attended by a large company of notable friends from among the clergy and laity, and were held in the church of which he had been the life and inspiration for many years. A company of young men from his Mount Hermon School, twelve on a side, bore his body a half mile down the main street of the village, followed by his co-worker, the famous singer, and others long associated with him in his work, with the trustees of his schools and his distinguished friends in their wake. The precious burden was laid down in front of the pulpit from which he had so often preached the riches of Christ with his wonted tenderness and power.

It was a cloudless December day, and during the services the slanting rays of the afternoon sun shot through the unstained windows and rested upon his quiet face, as if it were the smile of his Father attesting to the faithfulness of His servant.

Upon the conclusion of the service in the church, the casket was borne by his student-bearers, followed—with heavy feet and saddened hearts—by his devoted and admiring friends to the place pre-

pared for him on "Round Top," from which he
had expressed the wish to "rise from there on the
resurrection morning."

As the last rites were spoken and his form was
being lowered to its final resting place, the sun
was sinking behind the western hills—a coincidence
most impressive—an emblem, it seemed, strikingly
reminding us that night falls upon every day, yet
not one of despair, for as the sun marches on to
its rising in the morning, so will the great evangel
of "Love," like all who fall asleep in Him who is
Himself the resurrection and the life, rise again
when the morning "dawns and the shadows flee
away." The fact also that the central figure of
his generation in the religious history of his country was passing from the stage as the last rays of
the sun were fading upon the closing hours of
the century in which his great work was wrought
added impressiveness to the scene.

"Round Top" has become associated in the minds
of Christians the world over with "Northfield." It
is on the Seminary campus, well covered with trees
that give refreshing shade, and beautiful for situation. It is about three hundred yards directly
north of, and on the same level with, the house
in which he was born, and about the same distance

east of the home in which he spent the last twenty-five years of his life. At the place where the sunset services were held—and still are—is a depression, amphitheater in shape, sloping to the east; on the west a gentle slope toward his home and the river beyond, and on the north an abrupt descent from the top of which may be seen one of the most beautiful river, valley, hill and mountain views in New England.

Mr. Moody loved the place, as it was attractive to children in their play; and here, during the summer conferences, he was accustomed to gather the people in an informal way about him at sunset, before the evening services.

At the head of his grave stands a plain granite stone, upon which has been inscribed the following:

DWIGHT LYMAN MOODY
1837—1899
"He that doeth the will of God abideth forever."

By his side rests his gifted and faithful wife—a stone similar to that of her husband marking her resting place.

Thus passed from view the man who was the greatest blessing and inspiration to me of any that ever crossed my path; for it was he who opened the door of service and privilege, over the threshold of which—but for him—I would never have been able to pass. Nor would my life have been enriched by the many years of his fellowship or blessed by association with the noble men enlisted with him in the great campaign for God, of which he was the militant leader.

PROSPECTIVE

As I look back over the more than half century since Mr. Sankey became the pioneer of "Evangelistic Singers," it is most interesting and surprising to realize what a great army of consecrated men and women has arisen from that small beginning. And while I have seen my contemporaries drop out of the ranks one by one, my mind has been turned to those who have taken their places, and it is very encouraging to see such a number of talented musicians, writers and singers among them.

Instead of two or three singers and leaders, as was true when I joined the ranks threescore years ago, there are so many now that it would be difficult to enumerate them. Of the writers and their songs, there are those of the present day whose names will go down the years as being among the most illustrious in the annals of Christian song.

It has not been my privilege to know all of these, personally, as they belong to another generation, but I know them by "their works," and freely accord them the place they have so well merited.

The most outstanding figure among them, however, is he whom I have had in recent years the honor to count among my friends. I refer to Mr. Charles H. Gabriel, who has been acknowledged to be the most gifted and brilliant writer of Gospel songs during the last twoscore years.

He is, therefore, not far removed from the generation of early writers, with whose names his has been engraved on the hearts of the people, and upon the scroll of fame.

It would seem, however, that he stands to-day midway between that illustrious company and the writers of the present time, and that he has many years yet to "make the songs for the people," and to bless the world with his delightful and heart-appealing melodies.

He is the author of "The Glory Song," "He Lifted Me," and "The Sparrow Song," so much used by Mr. Alexander in all parts of the world.

Mr. E. O. Excell used to say, "It is to Gabriel's songs—'Hail Emmanuel,' 'He Is So Precious to Me,' 'The Way of the Cross,' and many others— I owe so much for any success I have gained." Mr. Rodeheaver also bore witness to the value of his compositions when he said, "Without 'Brighten the Corner,' 'Sail On,' 'My Wonderful Dream,' and 'Awakening Chorus'—not to mention others— I could not have held the immense choirs and tremendous audiences I have had to quiet and control."

His song, "Higher Ground," is sung universally, and I regard it as one of the privileges of my later life to have known him and to have come under the influence of his genial and kindly personality; and also to receive from him tokens of friendship and cordial regard I value beyond estimation.

That the future may deal kindly with Charles H. Gabriel, that his gifted pen may be used to enrich the field of sacred song for generations yet to come is the prayer of his host of friends and admirers. In this prayer I would include all those who are led and inspired of God to devote their gifts to this important field of service.

Of the noted leaders of recent years two, whose preëminence has had world-wide recognition—

Charles M. Alexander and Homer A. Rodeheaver
—come at once to the mind of every one. Of the
former, who has but recently been called to sing
anew the "Glory Song" among the redeemed in
the "land beyond the sea," reference has been made.

The latter is still with us and in the prime of
his manhood, waving his magic wand over great
congregations. I have met him but a few times, yet
this brief contact was sufficient for me to discover
his great gift as a leader and to be impressed by
the ease with which he controls vast multitudes of
people; also his winsome personality which ren-
ders him a worthy and invaluable associate of the
great evangelist with whom he has been working
for many years, in an endeavor to "Brighten the
Corner" in the heart of a world so much in need
of the light of the Gospel.

The great service of song, as it has been used
in evangelistic movements, was without question
called forth providentially to be used as a hand-
maid to the preaching of the Word, as has been
attested throughout its history, by the seal of God's
approval.

The enduring work of the pioneers in the ministry of song, very evidently, was wrought in God;
and though they have passed to their reward, "their

works do follow them." While this is true of them, it will be true of the present-day writers, leaders and singers; for we cannot doubt that God will raise up worthy successors to those who labor to-day when they—in turn—lay down the armor. The ranks of God's militant army will never be depleted! We should, therefore, not despair when we see great leaders fall at the sound of taps blown for them by order of the Great Commander-in-Chief.

THE END